A MacBrayne Album

A MacBrayne Album

ALISTAIR DEAYTON & IAIN QUINN

AMBERLEY

First published 2009

Amberley Publishing Plc
Cirencester Road, Chalford,
Stroud, Gloucestershire, GL6 8PE

www.amberley-books.com

Copyright © Alistair Deayton & Iain Quinn, 2009

The right of Alistair Deayton & Iain Quinn to be
identified as the Authors of this work has been asserted
in accordance with the Copyrights, Designs and
Patents Act 1988.
ISBN 978 1 84868 428 7

British Library Cataloguing in Publication Data.
A catalogue record for this book is available from the
British Library.

Typeset in 10 on 12pt Sabon.
Typesetting by Amberley Publishing.
Printed in the UK.

Contents

Acknowledgements

The authors greatly appreciate the help both in words and photographs from Robin Boyd, himself a lifelong MacBrayne enthusiast and honorary president of the Clyde River Steamer Club.

The late captain Alex F. Rodger was in life a Cape Horner, a Clyde steamer captain and enthusiast and a native of Jordanhill, where he lived in Achray Avenue. His glass slides have returned to Achray Avenue, fifty years after they were taken to Canada. The slides were flown back to the UK and transferred to PS Waverley in London and steamed to Glasgow on her light voyage home in the autumn of 2000. Alex was, in retirement, a respected figure and was honorary president of the CRSC until his passing in the early 1970s.

We thank Mr David Smith for the use of colours pictures taken by his late uncle, John Smith, a noted river enthusiast.

We would like to put on record the hard work of the captains and crew both in fair and foul weather. Without them all the isles of the Hebrides would be so much worse off.

Most of the illustrations are being aired for the first time and cover MacBrayne proper – in other words no lions on the funnels. A few of the illustrations appeared in various editions of Duckworth and Langmuir's West Highland Steamers, but appear here in a better reproduction due to modern scanning technology. There are also a handful that appeared in black and white in MacBrayne Steamers by co-author Alistair Deayton, and which appear here in colour.

Thanks are also due to the late, Graham E Langmuir, I.N. Mallinson, A.E. Glen, John Smith, C.L.D. Duckworth, the Mitchell Library, Angus Johnston, and Douglas Brown, to Archie McCallum, archivist of the Clyde River Steamer Club for use of the Duckworth notebooks, also to Caroline Edelin for the photo of the window in Christ Church, East Sheen, and to Campbell McCutcheon of Amberley Publishing for the images used on the cover.

Thanks finally to Derek Crawford of Gourock whose suitable words in the foreword are acknowledged. We hope you enjoy our book.

Alistair Deayton
Iain Quinn
September 2009

Foreword

At the launch of the Lochfyne at Denny's in early 1931, the comment was made by the chairman of the shipbuilder's that MacBrayne was more than just a business. It was a romance that recalled for all Scots the idea of Tir nan Og, the land of eternal youth, and stirred up passions of a bygone age of Celtic culture. What he alluded to was the area of Scotland that was considered to be forever MacBrayne; the West Coast and islands of Scotland. However, to those of us interested in the ships that have over the years plied the Clyde and Hebridean sea routes, the description could equally be used to describe the vessels of David MacBrayne and now Caledonian MacBrayne

If ever a company and a geographical area were synonymous it has to be MacBraynes and the West Coast community. From the dawn of steam to the age of the drive-through car ferry, the Company and its predecessors have been the life-blood of the area. All food and supplies, tourists, the islanders, their produce and even the components of their buildings have been carried to and fro by the red funnelled steamers; the domination of the red funnel was such that the novelist Neil Munro, born on Loch Fyneside, admitted that virtually until manhood he assumed every ship in the world had red and black funnels. The ships have carried out their lawful occasions through horrendous weather, economic downturn, war and political interference, maintaining the essential links to and from the islands.

Many books have been produced over the years on the Company and its vessels and many might wonder why another is required. Well, why not if the story is worth retelling. The vast bulk of the photographs in this book were taken by respected enthusiasts of the previous generation and have been brought together by two well known names of the present. The vast majority have not been in the public domain before and provide a fascinating window into the mod twentieth century chapter of the MacBrayne story. Their publication provides an important link in the story for both enthusiasts and historians and are a fitting tribute to all those connected with the Company over the years for their efforts in maintaining such an efficient service to meet the needs of the public.

Derek Crawford

Introduction

In 1851 G.&J. Burns sold their West Highland steamers services to David Hutcheson & Co. One of the conditions of the sale was that Hutcheson take on David MacBrayne, a nephew of the Burns brothers, as a junior partner. When David Hutcheson retired in 1878, David MacBrayne, at the age of sixty-five, took the company over and renamed it. Ever since MacBraynes has been an integral part of life in the West Highlands and islands of Scotland, since 1973 as part of Caledonian MacBrayne.

At the heart of this book is a collection of glass slides and glass-mounted medium format negatives donated in recent years to Iain Quinn. These had originally belonged to Captain Alex Rodger, but in the meantime had been to Canada and back. These have been augmented by items from the collections of the authors, and from a couple of notebooks from C.L.D. Duckworth, which are in the archive of the Clyde River Steamer Club.

Special attention is given to four steamers, *Columba*, the premier paddle steamer operating in UK waters, *Iona*, her predecessor on the Royal Route from Glasgow to Ardrishaig, and which had a remarkably long life of seventy-one years, and the two turbine steamers, *Saint Columba*, which succeeded *Columba* on the Royal Route, and *King George V*, which made the Staffa and Iona cruise from Oban her own from 1936 to 1974.

The other paddle and screw steamers in the fleet are not ignored, neither are the motor vessels, which were used by MacBrayne from the early 1900s onwards, and the 'wee red boats' which tendered to the larger vessels at ports without a pier, particularly at Staffa and Iona. This is the story of the MacBrayne fleet prior to the era of the car ferry, so the 1964 car ferry trio are omitted

By the 1920s, MacBraynes owned an assortment of old steamers, said by some to be a veritable museum of steamship history. 1927 was their *annus horribilis*, when *Sheila* ran aground in the early hours of New Years Day entering Stornoway, *Chevalier* ran aground on Barmore Island in Loch Fyne on 25 March, and *Grenadier* was destroyed by fire whilst lying at Oban on 5 September. This tipped the company to the verge of bankruptcy and they did not bid for the mail contract in the following year. In 1928 the government intervened and a new company, David MacBrayne (1928), was formed, jointly owned by Coast Lines and the London Midland & Scottish Railway. This joint ownership continued until 1969 when the Scottish Transport Group was formed and took over Coast Lines' 50 per cent. The Railway Company had been nationalised in 1948, and the railway shipping operations in Scotland were transferred to the Scottish Transport Group on 1 January 1969. In 1973 David MacBrayne and the Caledonian Steam Packet Co. merged to form Caledonian MacBrayne.

1936 saw the purchase of the Williamson-Buchanan fleet by the LMSR, and the two steamers in that fleet, operated by Turbine Steamers Ltd, came to MacBraynes. *Queen*

Alexandra of 1912 was rebuilt with a third funnel and renamed *Saint Columba*, serving the Glasgow and Gourock to Ardrishaig route until 1958, while *King George V* was little altered and went to the Sacred Isle cruise from Oban round Mull to Staffa and Iona, where she became a great favourite until withdrawn in 1972.

Chapter 1

Tales of an Edwardian Passenger

Recently discovered are a couple of loose-leaf notebooks compiled by C.L.D. Duckworth in 1925. They contain the core material which was reproduced in *West Highland Steamers*, co-authored with Graham E. Langmuir. They also contain a number of notes on journeys on MacBrayne steamers, pre-1914, hand-written on MacBrayne notepaper. Duckworth was born in 1891 so would have been aged between nineteen and twenty-two when these were written.

RMS Grenadier
Sat Jan 29th 1910

Greenock-Ardrishaig-Greenock

We left Princes Pier, Greenock about 9.15 a.m. It was a magnificent day although very cold. The snow-clad hills were very effective. I had breakfast between Gourock and Dunoon. The "Grenadier" is 356 ton, paddle, two cyl compound oscillating engine. Her summer service is round Mull but she always takes the Ardrishaig mails in the winter. We called at the customary places: Gourock, Dunoon, Innellan, Rothesay, Colintraive, Tighnabruaich Tarbert and Ardrishaig. We passed the "Fingal" nr Tighnabruaich. Reached Ardrishaig about 1.15. Mr & Mrs MacMillan were very pleased to see me at the Pier. Unfortunately the steamer only stayed a few minutes. I went into dock with her at Greenock where we berthed at 6 p.m. A most delightful sail. Superb Day.

RMS Iona, Linnet and Chevalier
Monday July 25th 1910

Wemyss Bay-Ardrishaig-Crinan-Oban

I left for my tour at 10.40 from Wemyss Bay on the "Iona". We called only at Tighnabruaich on the way to Ardrishaig and there were only 14 other passengers besides myself! MacMillan and his wife met me on the pier, which was crowded with those coming south. The "Linnet" was not full. The "Comet" was in the canal (to be used in case of pressure). A good many people walked during the series of locks about Cairnbaan. Everything much the same as usual. Weather, inclined to rain, which it did before Oban. There was quite a sea in the "Chevalier" in some parts. My cap blew overboard, but luckily I had another. The "Chevalier" pitched slightly, but is a good sea boat (2 cyl simple engine). The "Linnet" has diags 2 cyl simple twin scr engines. We get to Oban about 5.15 p.m.

RMS Gael
Tuesday July 26th 1910

Oban-Gairloch

We left Oban at 7 a.m. Weather not good, but improving by degrees. A light NW wind kept the sea on the move, and that when we rounded Ardnamurchan Pt we pitched considerably and rolled later on by Eigg. The "Glencoe" came into Mallaig as we left and the "Claymore" also. A boat came out in a good many calls where there was no pier. We stayed some time at Kyle, & again at Portree, so that we were ½ hr late at Gairloch, where we arrived at 8 p.m., 13 hours from Oban. The last piece between Portree and Gairloch was very fine, with the setting sun, deep blue water of the Minch, with a low Atlantic swell gently heaving. Outer Hebrides fairly visible. The machinery of "Gael" is worth a special note 2 cyl simple oscillating engines with 5 1/3 ft stroke and double piston rods. The chief told me she was very difficult to start from certain positions and frequently got stuck. The link motion worked abominably badly with jerks and kicks in all directions. Stokeholds in one with the engines. The port cylinder was new this year after the accident of blowing a cover out last year. The seaworthiness of the ship is undeniable, for she behaved admirably off Ardnamurchan, without 'racing' at all. She is certainly a tougher boat than most of the paddle steamers, although very old.

RMS Gairlochy
RMS Mountaineer
Thursday July 28th 1910

Inverness-Banavie-Fort William-Oban

Had an early breakfast at 6 a.m. and left at 6.30 for the Canal. The "Gairlochy" sailed at 7 a.m. Steeple engine, 1 cyl., 4 piston rods, very slow and rickety! Fine weather to Banavie where it rained heavily. The "Glengarry" was at Inverness – we passed the "Lochness". Fine views are visible on Loch Ness and Loch Lochy. Arr. Banavie 3 p.m. NBR engine No.19 4-4-0T took us to Fort William (5 miles). We got the new "Mountaineer" then to Oban. She is a very curiously built boat. Engines similar to "Pioneer". 2 cyl sv compound, my first. She it was which I watched being built this year at Pointhouse yard. Wet most of the way. The "Handa" was in Oban. I hadn't seen her for a very long time – and also the "Lochiel". We got to Oban at 6.10 p.m.

RMS Lochawe
RMS Iona
RMS Columba
Saturday July 30th 1910

Oban-Loch Awe-Ardrishaig-Rothesay-Wemyss Bay

Train left Oban at 7.05 a.m. with C Ry engines No.58 & 196 4-4-0 and 4-6-0 express. Pouring rain and very nasty. The "Lochawe" sailed at 9 o'clock. She is quite a nice steamer with 2 cyl simple engines with exhaust up funnel. White Hull and pink bottom. Rain all the way to Ford. Fast and noisy on to Ardrishaig, passing a house which the Jollys had one year. At Ardrishaig I met the MacMillans and they gave me tea at

Auchnagiach. The "Columba" was late and had time to stay a bit with them and it was very good of them to have me. The "Columba" left an hour late at 2 p.m. and I went to Rothesay in her and then changed into the "Iona" for Wemyss Bay, where I arrived at 6 p.m. The weather was bad practically all the way from Oban. Crowd on the "Columba" the only one throughout the whole tour.

RMS Columba
RMS Linnet
RMS Mountaineer
Sat 13th 1911

Glasgow-Ardrishaig-Crinan-Oban

Arthur and I left Bridge Wharf at 7.10 a.m. Delightful day with bright sun. Not too many passengers. Reached Ardrishaig at 1 o'clock and met Mr & Mrs Macmillan, than sailed to Crinan in the "Linnet", then had the new "Mountaineer " to Oban, the "Chevalier" being off for the winter now. Arthur had not seen any of the scenery for over 5 years. Oban was very busy, the Regatta and Gathering being on. Crowds. Since the hotels were full we arranged to sleep aboard the island steamer and to sailing next morning for Tobermory.

RMS Iona
Sat Aug 24th 1912

Wemyss Bay-Ardrishaig

We sailed from Wemyss Bay shortly after 6 p.m. It was a fine evening, but not much view. After a high tea I found we were near Rothesay. Calls made at Colintraive, Tighnabruaich, Auchenlochan, Kames and Tarbert. It was pretty dark after Ardlamont Point. Ettrick Bay was visible. Da burnt a Roman Candle as we passed the house. Arrived at 9.00 p.m. The "Iona" was going well. This was the first time I had sailed up Loch Fyne at night, and it was most enjoyable. Dead calm up here. A's friend Lloyd is the only guest up here now, they met me at the pier.

RMS Iona
Wednesday Oct 9th 1912

Gourock-Ardrishaig-Gourock

Left the Central at 8.15 a.m. for Gourock, We sailed at 9.20 a.m. Had breakfast immediately. It was a chilly day and misty. Both Cloch and Toward horns were blowing. The sun came out shortly. Very few passengers. We made the usual calls and reached Ardrishaig at 12.50. Mt & Mrs MacMillan were on the pier and we had 10 minutes talk. The expressed their grief at our departure. The house is now in the hands of bad caretakers and will soon be filthy. Everything was beginning to wear a wintry aspect, and very different form the summer. I wrote several letters on board. It was pleasant to get away today although rather solitary being alone. Arrived at Central 5.35 –very good time. This completes my trips for the year.

RMS Chevalier
Sat February 1st 1913

<u>Gourock-Ardrishaig</u>
I left the Central at 8.30 a.m. to join the steamer for Ardrishaig, en route to the Hunters at Lochgilphead. Was surprised to find the "Chevalier" running; but the "Grenadier" had broken her shaft. Yesterday, I hear the "Fusilier" had to be put on as the "Chev" was temporarily disabled. It was a wild day, but evidently not as bad as yesterday. Snow lying everywhere. We shipped seas between Tighnabruaich and Tarbert rounding Ardlamont Point and had a list to starboard. Rain at intervals and awfully cold. Few passengers. We were 95 mins late at Ardrishaig. Frank Hunter met me in their small car. I wrote to Elspeth on board. The "Iona's" engineer was in charge. Capt MacMillan on the bridge. We had lunch on arrival at Lochgilphead.

RMS Columba
Wed August 13th 1913

<u>Glasgow-Ardrishaig</u>
Arthur and I got up at 6 a.m. and drive to the Central to pick up part of our baggage. Met Da on board and he sailed down the river with us. We left at 7.11 a.m. The Clyde yards seemed busy. Fairfield was full in the yard as far as I could see. Mother and the remainder of the party, consisting of cats, servants, and baggage got on at Gourock. Rain for portions of the journey. Route as usual, not many passengers. We arrived in good time and found the two nice McEwan girls on the pier, seeing a friend off.

RMS Grenadier
New Year's Day 1914

<u>Gourock-Ardrishaig</u>
Left Central at 8.40 a.m. for Gourock after a small breakfast in Sutherland St at 7.30. "Grenadier" full of people and ½ hour late in starting. Mild day – very different to the earlier part of the week. Scarcely a breath of wind. Everything as usual here. Saloon decorated with holly and ship was lighted electrically. MacMillan on the pier to meet me. Crowd waiting to see the steamer arrive, even more than in the summer! Somehow I feel out of place being here on a New Year's Day! Vehicle was waiting for me and I drive straight to Inverneill. Remarkable calmness of the sea for the season.

RMS Columba, Linnet, Mountaineer, Fusilier, Gondolier
Grenadier to Staffa and Iona
12-14/7/1927

<u>Glasgow to Inverness via Crinan and Caledonian Canals</u>
(No notes for this trip)

Chapter 2

West Highland Shipowners

From *Memoirs and Portraits of One Hundred Glasgow Men* by James MacLehose, 1886.

From the entry for James Burns (1789-1871).

One famous line the Burns's worked up, and then, under the pressure of greater enterprises, abandoned. This was the Royal Route (well-named) through the West Highlands. The Crinan route got the name of the "Royal Route", from its having been used by the Queen on her visit to Scotland in 1847. She was sent that way by the glowing account she had of it from the Grand Duke Constantine, who, on a visit to Scotland the year before, had been sent that way by the Admiralty. They began the Highland trade about 1832, and in 1835 bought three little steamers, the "Rob Roy", the "Helen Macgregor", and the "Inverness", which William Young, a plumber, had been running to little profit through the Crinan. From this beginning they worked up a whole system of steamers for the day passage through the Crinan or the night passage round the Mull, gliding along canals or battling with the Atlantic, meeting at Oban, crossing and re-crossing, plunging into the lochs, winding along the sounds, threading their way among the islands, fine pleasure boats for the flock of summer swallows, stout trading boats summer and winter serving the whole archipelago, linking with the world the lonely bay or the outer islet, freighted out with supplies of all sorts and shapes, freighted in with wool and sheep, Highland beasts and Highland bodies: surely the liveliest service in the world! But they had their hands more than full, and in 1851 they handed over the whole fleet to the new firm of David Hutcheson & Co., consisting of David Hutcheson, who had been with them from the old smack days; his brother, Alexander Hutcheson, who had also been with them; and their nephew, David MacBrayne. There has been many a change since then in the service. Fairy steamers have replaced the Crinan track boats of our youth and the boys galloping in their scarlet jackets: the "Iona" and the "Columba", the "Clansman" and the "Claymore" – we had not dreamt of such vessels: in every detail there have been vast improvements. But in all its main features the service is as the Burns's made it. To their initiative, which others have ably followed up, thousands of travellers from all parts owe the most delightful of their travels – thousands of ourselves, worn by the strain of the town, owe the new life sucked in with the breath of the heather, the music of the ocean, the untold delights of the West Highlands.

David Hutcheson (1799-1880).
Born in Inverkeithing, Fife, Hutcheson's family moved west where his father established a cooperage in Port Glasgow but soon died. Hutcheson worked his way up through the shipping trade, eventually becoming a manager and partner at the Burns shipping company, which initially mainly operated steamers between the Clyde and Liverpool. In

1851, by which time the company owned ocean-going vessels, the steamers were sold to the MacBrayne brothers, for whom Hutcheson now worked. The company leased the island of Staffa in the interests of the tourist trade, and sailed as far north as Lochinver, Hutcheson died in Glasgow but was buried between Oban and Dunstaffnage. An obelisk was built in his memory on Kerrera.

DAVID HUTCHESON was born at Inverkeithing in 1799. His parents soon after went to reside in Port-Glasgow, where his father carried on the business of a cooperage. Here his father died, leaving David at an early age to the care of a widowed mother, a conscientious Scottish woman, who in the midst of a hard struggle gave him the rudiments of a sound education, which in his early manhood he improved and extended by his own application and love of knowledge.

His first employment was that of a clerk in Steel's cooperage in Port-Glasgow. Leaving that situation in 1817, he entered the service of a shipping firm who were owners of two small luggage steamboats, named the "Industry" and the "Trusty", which carried goods between Glasgow, Port-Glasgow, and Greenock. Mr Hutcheson continued in this position for several years, and subsequently transferred his services to the Glasgow and Leith Shipping Company at Port-Dundas, and afterwards to Mr Kid, the agent of Messrs Mathie & Thixton, who were owners of a line of Liverpool smacks. Mr Kid dying soon afterwards, the Messrs Burns succeeded to the agency, and assumed Mr Hutcheson as manager, with a share in the profits.

Mr Hutcheson's connection with the Messrs Burns lasted till 1851, when the firm, who by that time had become a great Ocean Steam Navigation Company, sold the whole of their steamers engaged in the Highland carrying trade to Mr Hutcheson, his brother Alexander, and Mr David MacBrayne.

Since the completion of the Caledonian Canal in 1822, the trade of the West Highlands had been gradually developing, but the steamers were of a small class, with limited accommodation. The new firm at once began to replace these by others of a different description, and in 1852 the "Mountaineer" was built, the first of the grand steamers on the Ardrishaig route, and the precursor of the present magnificent fleet of mail steamers to the Western Highlands. Following the "Mountaineer" came three steamers, each called the "Iona". The first two, after running between Glasgow and Ardrishaig for several years, were sold to the American Confederate Government, and both, strange to say, were wrecked on the outward voyage: one being run down by a screw steamship between Roseneath and Fort Matilda, while the other foundered off the English coast. In 1864, the third "Iona" was placed on the station, and her fame became world-wide. She runs now between Crinan and Banavie, her place on the Ardrishaig route being supplied by the "Columba", a steamer which has far surpassed any of her predecessors, and which may be described as unrivalled either in the Old or New World as regards speed, comfort, and elegance.

While developing the traffic between Glasgow and Ardrishaig, Mr Hutcheson and his partners were at the same time extending their enterprise among the Western Hebrides, and along the northern coast of the island. They leased the Island of Staffa to secure the public from interruption in viewing the wonders of Fingal's Cave, and establishing a fleet of well-appointed steamers between Oban, Iona, Mull, Skye, the Lewis, and the small ports lying along the north-west coast, as far north as Loch Inver, gave an impulse to the whole trade of the West Highlands. Oban, from being an unattractive, insignificant village, has become a great centre of tourists. Villages and villa residences have sprung up everywhere, and what is probably the grandest picturesque country in the world has been opened up, not merely to the thousands who inhabit our crowded cities, but to the traveller and the tourist from every quarter of the globe.

It is almost impossible to estimate the amount of good which has been conferred on the Highlands by the enterprise of the firm of which Mr Hutcheson was the moving spirit. Not only has the value of property been increased, but the blessings of social improvement have been brought within the reach of the thousands who people the shores of its beautiful bays and lochs, who also enjoy the advantage of convenient and economical intercourse between their once remote hamlets and the great centres of industry: benefits which will extend to the Highlands of the future a prosperity far more real and enduring that can ever be attained through the varied philosophies of Land and Socialistic Reform.

This is not the place to speak of Mr Hutcheson otherwise than as an energetic man of business; but we cannot refrain from saying that in private life he was esteemed by a large circle of friends, many of whom were distinguished for their high position in the world of letters and art, who appreciated his worth and varied abilities.

He was a man of refined culture, courteous and genial, alike to the prince and the peasant; a lover of literature; a liberal patron of the fine arts; fond of music, and an enthusiastic admirer of our great national bard, whose songs and poems he used to sing and recite. Few who had the pleasure of meeting him socially could forget his rendering of the "Wee, Wee German Lairdie", or "Tam o' Shanter," or his favourite song, "Farewell to Lochaber," a district which he dearly loved. Himself a poet of no mean rank, it is a great satisfaction to his friends that the desire breathed in one of his poems some years ago has been realized:

> For I would wish my bones to lie
> Among the scenes I loved so well;
> The mountain glen, the gorgeous sky,
> The wimpling burn, the gowany dell.
> And where were sepulchre more sweet
> For me than 'mong dear Oban's braes,
> Where oft in contemplation sweet
> I, rambling, tuned my simple lays.

The wish was not disregarded; and when he died, in his eighty-second year, his remains were brought from Glasgow and interred in the picturesque cemetery of Peny-friar, between Oban and Dunstaffnage Castle.

His fellow-citizens and the leading inhabitants of the West of Scotland felt that some memorial of Mr Hutcheson's worth and public service should be preserved, and, after much consideration, a monumental obelisk was erected on the Island of Kerrera, and now forms a conspicuous feature in the scenery of Oban Bay.

Mr Hutcheson was married early in life to Miss Dawson, a lady of a family well known both in Glasgow and Linlithgow, who died May 16th, 1885. Without drawing aside the veil which encloses the domestic circle, we know we speak the sentiments of all who ever entered their hospitable mansion, when we say that in her Mr Hutcheson had for his long-life-partner one of kindred tastes and aspirations.

Above left: David Hutcheson

Above right: David MacBrayne

THE LATE DAVID MacBRAYNE From *Who's Who in Glasgow 1908.*

THE man to whom the Hebrides and Western Highlands of Scotland owed more than to any one else in his time was without doubt Mr David MacBrayne. Everywhere among the sea-lochs and islands of the West Coast the steamers of his famous fleet are welcomed as the connecting link with the civilization and comforts of the greater world. It is by these steamers that the sons and daughters of the West go off to find their fortunes in a wider sphere, and by these steamers is brought back the eagerly looked for news of their prosperity, with their kindly gifts, to the remotest clachans and shielings of the isles. By these steamers, too, all summer long, the tourist wealth of the south is poured throughout the Hebrides, and all the year through the products of the isles are carried away to be converted into the things desired. It is proof of the kindly manner in which this enterprise has been carried on, that in all these years no rival has ever found a footing in the western seas, and that the invasion by railways at important points has only increased the steamers' trade.

A native of Glasgow, where he was born over ninety years ago, Mr MacBrayne was a grandson of Dr Burns of the Barony Church, whose two sons established the great steamship company of G.&J. Burns. The story of his steamboat enterprise forms one of the romances of commerce. In 1842 a group of Glasgow merchants, among whom were W. Campbell of Tilliechewan. J. Hunter of Hafton, and A.S. Finlay of Castle Toward, entered on passenger steamer ownership on the Clyde by building the *Duntroon Castle*.

From the names of the various steamers it put upon the water the association was known as the Castle Company. But it did not succeed, and in 1845 the steamers were sold to Messrs G.&J. Burns. The new owners at once attempted to "corner" the Clyde steamboat traffic, and for a time ran passengers to any point of their vessels' call for the sum of twopence. The effort, however, did not produce any adequate result, and in 1848 the ownership was devolved upon the firm of David Hutcheson & Co. The devolution was a family arrangement, David and Alexander Hutcheson being closely related to the Messrs Burns, and Mr MacBrayne, the junior partner, their nephew. Already there was a considerable traffic with the West Highlands through the Crinan Canal by track-boat, and from Crinan to Oban by the steamer *Brenda*. In August, 1847, Queen Victoria had travelled by this route to the West Highlands and it had thus acquired the name of the Royal Route. This traffic the Messrs Hutcheson rapidly developed, buying the *Shandon* and other steamers from the previous owners, Thomson & M'Connell, and building their "crack" steamer, the first *Iona*, in 1855. Seven years later she was sold to run the American blockade, but was sunk off Fort Matilda by the *Chanticleer. Iona* No.2, built in the following year, was also sold for the blockade, but sank on her way thither, off Lundy Island. In 1864 the present *Iona* was built, and carried on the tradition of the "crack" steamer's name.

David Hutcheson retired from the business in 1876, and by the retiral of Alexander Hutcheson two years later Mr MacBrayne was left sole owner of the fleet. He inaugurated his control with the building of the *Columba* in 1878, and so regained the supremacy on the Clyde which had been threatened by the launch of the *Lord of the Isles*. To-day the MacBrayne fleet consists of thirty-three steamers manned by more than a thousand officers and men, to say nothing of some five hundred employees on shore. Outside the Clyde the vessels ply to every port and island, from Islay to Thurso, and perform a service only differing in degree from that of the Cunard fleet of Mr MacBrayne's cousin, Lord Inverclyde.

Of a somewhat retiring disposition, Mr MacBrayne never courted public life, but among his duties as a citizen he was long an officer of volunteers, passing through all the grades from ensign to major. He was for several years a member of the Clyde Trust, and he was on the Commission of the Peace for the County of Lanark. Latterly his two sons, Mr David Hope and Mr Laurence MacBrayne, relieved him of the more burdensome details of business management, and about a year before his death the firm was converted into a limited liability company, with Mr David Hope MacBrayne as its chairman; but the veteran owner to the last kept in touch both with the affairs and with the personnel of his splendid fleet. Mr MacBrayne died at his residence in Glasgow on 26th January, 1907.

Chapter 3

RMS *Columba* and *Iona*

Columba was the premier paddle steamer in UK waters, and the longest ever Clyde steamer. Her route from Glasgow to Ardrishaig took the upper classes to their shooting lodges in the West Highlands as well as day excursionists from Glasgow, Greenock and Gourock.

Duckworth writes:

The Queen of all paddle saloon passenger steamers. Mr MacBrayne made his debut with this ship and at once secured the premier position on the Clyde as owner of the finest specimen of marine architecture of her class and period.

Building her of steel was deemed a bold step. She was launched on 11/04/78.

With her on the Glasgow-Ardrishaig section of the "Royal Route" to 'Oban and the North' in summer the service progressed steadily and increased in popularity.

No steamer had better appointed or more commodious accommodation for both saloon and steerage passengers. She surpassed all others in beauty, size and speed and was and is a truly magnificent and dignified craft to behold. In the writer's opinion she eclipsed entirely the *Lord of the Isles*, her rival, in appearance.

Iona, her predecessor on the Ardrishaig route had the fifth longest career of any Clyde or West Highland steamer after *Glencoe*, *Glengarry*, *Gondolier* and *Dunara Castle*. She was the third steamer of that name, the previous two having been sold for Blockade Running in the US Civil War, although neither reached their destination. She inherited the deck saloons of her predecessor, and was noted for the old-fashioned design of these, which had a walkway between them and the side of the hull. After the introduction of *Columba*, she operated as a secondary steamer on the Ardrishaig run, from 1904 to 1914 running an express service from Wemyss Bay with two return trips daily. After the First World War, she spent time on the Lochgoilhead and Arrochar service, and after 1927, ran from Oban to Fort William.

Both were withdrawn after the 1935 summer season and were scrapped during the following year at Arnott Young, Dalmuir.

Columba arriving at Gourock.

Columba at speed off the Cowal Coast.

Columba, with naval vessels in the background, in Rothesay Bay.

The engine of *Columba*. This was a two cylinder simple oscillating engine.

Columba in East India Harbour, Greenock, with *Comet* berthed alongside.

Columba in dry dock at Govan in 1935 prior to her final season. A similar photo appeared in the Glasgow newspaper, *The Bulletin*.

The paddle box of *Columba* being dismantled at Arnott Young's at Dalmuir in 1936. Most of the rest of the steamer is already gone. Note the thistle growing out of the letter U, part of the design that was not normally visible.

IONA (I) — 1855-1862

A fictitious painting of *Iona* of 1855 passing the island of Iona. She was never there in her short career, which was spent entirely on the Glasgow to Ardrishaig service. After only eight seasons in service she was sold for blockade running, but was run down off Gourock on her delivery voyage. Unlike her successors of the name she was flush-decked.

A second *Iona* was built in 1863, this time with deck saloons, but was sold after her first season, and sank off Lundy on 2 February 1864. A replacement was ordered as soon as she was sold, and the third *Iona* entered service for the summer season of 1864. She is seen here at speed in the Firth of Clyde.

Iona arriving at Gourock.

Iona arriving at Rothesay, showing the gilt scrollwork on the bow surrounding the name.

Iona berthing at Dunoon.

A well-filled *Iona* arriving at
Rothesay.

A stern view of *Iona* in
Rothesay Bay, showing the gilt
scrollwork on the stern and
the bridge between the funnels
which was added in the 1870-
71 winter refit.

Iona at Tighnabruaich, in her pre-1871 condition, prior to her funnels being heightened.

Iona going astern out of Tarbert, Loch Fyne.

Iona at Ardrishaig.

Iona at Corpach. From 1880 to 1885 she was on the Oban to Corpach service, connecting with the Caledonian Canal steamers to Inverness. This view shows the Chadburn telegraph on the bridge, which was added in 1873.

Iona in Loch Linnhe during the period from 1927 to 1935 when she was on the Oban to Fort William service.

Iona and *Lochfyne* at Fort William on an occasion when *Lochfyne* had broken down and *Iona* had been sent to relieve her. This was *Iona*'s final visit to Fort William.

Iona, with *Loch Broom* berthed ahead of her at Lancefield Quay, Glasgow. In the thirties, she took the Glasgow to Ardrishaig service for short spells in spring and autumn, before and after her Fort William season.

Chapter 4
Other Paddle Steamers

Glencoe was built in 1846 for service from Glasgow to Stornoway as *Mary Jane*. In 1851 she was sold to the Glasgow & Lochfine (*sic.*) Steam Packet Co. and in 1857 that company was taken over by David Hutcheson. She started on the Glasgow to Inveraray service and over the years ran on a number of MacBrayne routes. In November and December 1917 she was chartered to the GSWR for the Ardrossan to Arran service, and in spring 1918 was chartered to the CSP to operate out of Wemyss Bay. Following the war years she was on the Mallaig to Portree mail service until withdrawal and scrapping in 1931, at the venerable age of eighty-five. She is seen here off Kyle of Lochalsh.

Glencoe at Kyle of Lochalsh Railway Pier.

Glencoe at Corpach. From 1886 to 1889 she operated the Oban to Fort William and Corpach service.

Glencoe moored alongside *Lochfyne* in Glasgow on 4 June 1931, when the old and new vessels were open to the public as part of Glasgow Civic Week. *Glencoe* went to the breakers yard a few months later, aged eighty-five. Her steeple engine dated from 1846. After her scrapping the engine was presented to Glasgow Corporation, and lay in the basement of Kelvingrove Museum but was scrapped during the Second World War.

Right: Inveraray Castle was built in 1839 for the Glasgow to Inveraray cargo service, which she served all her life. In 1857 her owners were taken over by Hutcheson and she continued on the service until broken up in 1892.

Below: Chevalier was built in 1866, a smaller version of *Iona*. She mainly served the Crinan-Oban-Fort William-Corpach service but was on the Glasgow to Lochgoilhead and Arrochar service during part of 1913 and 1914. She was often on the Ardrishaig mail service in the winter months, and whist engaged on that service, met her end on 25 March 1927 when she ran aground on Barmore Island, Loch Fyne. She is seen here in Loch Fyne prior to 1901 when she was reboilered and she received new, fatter funnels.

Chevalier being broken up at Troon in 1927.

Chevalier arriving at Arrochar, with the wider funnels in 1913 or 1914.

Grenadier was built in 1885 and was closely associated with the Staffa and Iona sailing from Oban round Mull. She is seen here, in original condition with thin funnels, off Iona, with crew helping passengers out of the ferry boats.

Left: Grenadier anchored off Iona in her original condition, pre-1903.

Below: Grenadier anchored in the Sound of Iona in her later condition, post-1902.

Grenadier anchored off Staffa after alterations when she was reboilered in the 1902-03 winter. In this condition she was a most handsome steamer.

On the night of 5 September 1927, *Grenadier* was burnt out whilst lying at Oban with the loss of three lives. She is seen here having been prepared for the tow to be scrapped at Ardrossan, with her windows boarded up and pumps on board.

Fusilier was built in 1888 and operated out of Oban, mainly to Fort William and Corpach, where she is seen here with Ben Nevis, Britain's highest mountain, in the background. Note the horse-drawn coach waiting to convey passengers to Banavie, at the top of the flight of locks known as Neptune's Staircase, to connect with the Caledonian Canal steamers.

Fusilier in original condition with storm boards around her promenade deck, arriving at Onich, Loch Leven.

Fusilier, as altered with a heightened funnel and the bridge in front of the funnel, alterations which took place in 1926, arriving at Port Askaig, Islay.

Fusilier in her altered condition. In 1934 she was sold and operated in that year from the Firth of Forth and then from Llandudno under the names *Lady Orme* and *Crestawave* before being scrapped in 1939.

Above: Hero had been built for Clyde service in 1861, and was purchased by David MacBrayne in 1890. A couple of years later she was renamed *Mountaineer*. She was based at Oban in the summer months as an excursion steamer and is seen here off Dunollie entering Oban Bay. She was scrapped in 1909.

Left: Islay (III) was built in 1872 for the Stranraer to Larne service as *Princess Louise* and was purchased by MacBrayne in 1890 for the Glasgow to Islay service. She is seen here after running aground on Sheep Island, near Port Ellen, on 15 July 1902 in dense fog. This stranding proved fatal for her.

Lovedale was built in 1867 as *Great Western* for the Great Western Railway, and ran for them initially from Milford, now Milford Haven, to Waterford, and later from Weymouth to the Channel Islands. MacBrayne purchased her in 1891 and operated her from Strome Ferry to Stornoway. In 1893 she was reboiled, received the single funnel shown, in place of the previous two, and new paddle boxes and was renamed *Lovedale*. Following the opening of the railway to Kyle of Lochalsh in 1897 she sailed from there and in 1900 she moved to the Portree mail service, extended to Lochinver on summer Saturdays. In 1903 she was on the Glasgow to Islay service after the loss of *Islay*, and was broken up in 1904. She is seen here off Lochmaddy, North Uist.

Gael was another second-hand purchase in 1892. She was built in 1867 for the Campbeltown & Glasgow Steam Packet Joint Stock Co. Ltd for the Glasgow to Campbeltown service. In 1883 she was sold to the Great Western Railway for the Weymouth to the Channel Islands service. For MacBrayne she operated the summer thrice-weekly service for Oban to Gairloch. She is seen here leaving Oban in early MacBrayne condition, before the raised fo'csle was fitted in the early 1900s. Following the First World War she operated on various routes and was used as a director's yacht before being scrapped in 1924.

Gael, following the fitting of the raised fo'csle, laid up for the winter in Bowling Harbour, with *Mountaineer, Fusilier, Grenadier, Lord of the Isles,* five North British steamers and four Clyde Navigation Trust hoppers.

Carabinier was built in 1878 for the joint railways service from Portsmouth to the Isle of Wight as *Albert Edward* and was purchased by MacBrayne in October 1893. She spent her career on the Sound of Mull service from Tobermory to Oban until replaced by *Lochinvar* and sold for breaking up in 1908. She is seen here off Oban.

Glendale was another second-hand purchase, this time in 1902 as a replacement for
Islay (III) on the Glasgow to Islay service. She had been built in 1875 for the London,
Brighton & South Coast Railway's Newhaven to Dieppe service as *Paris*. She was sold
back to her builders, Fairfield, and in summer 1890 ran from Liverpool to North Wales,
and from 1892 to 1895 from Hamburg to Helgoland as *Flamingo* for Albert Ballin, owner
of the Hamburg-America Line. 1896 to 1902 saw her sailing from Tilbury to Ostend as
La Belgique. Initially in 1903 she was on the Oban to Gairloch route, *Gael* having gone
to the Stornoway mail service and *Lovedale* to the Islay route. She later moved to the
Stornoway route, and finally to the Glasgow to Islay service, where she was wrecked
on Deas Point on the Mull of Kintyre on 20 July 1905. She is seen here arriving at
Tobermory with *Claymore* in the background.

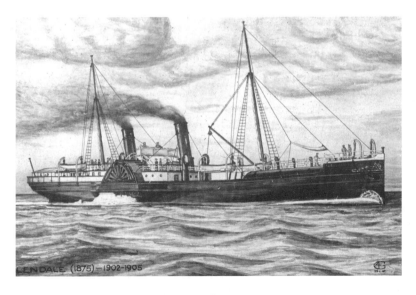

A drawing of *Glendale* by A. Ernest Glen, showing the unusual whale-backed fo'csle on
the foredeck.

Pioneer was built in 1905 for the West Loch Tarbert to Islay service and is seen here leaving West Loch Tarbert. She was due to be replaced in 1939 by the new *Lochiel*, but late-running alterations to the pier at West Loch Tarbert intervened and *Pioneer* continued in service until 1944, when she was requisitioned for the Admiralty. She was initially stationed at Fairlie as a Submarine Command HQ ship, and was later renamed HMS *Harbinger* in 1945. The following year her paddle wheels were removed and she was towed to Portland to be used as a floating laboratory until scrapped in 1958.

Another view of *Pioneer* departing West Loch Tarbert.

Mountaineer, the third of that name in the fleet, was built in 1910 for services from Oban, and is seen here departing Oban North Pier. In her first season she had solid bulwarks on the promenade deck as seen here.

Mountaineer arriving at Gourock when she was on the Loch Goil service, which was taken over by MacBrayne in 1912 from the Lochgoil & Inveraray Steamboat Co.

Mountaineer off Gourock.

Mountaineer with *Lochearn* behind her at Tobermory Games 1937. After the following season she was sold for scrapping.

Chapter 5
Caledonian Canal Steamers

Glengarry was built in 1844 as *Edinburgh Castle* for the service from Glasgow to the Holy Loch. Two years later she moved to the Caledonian Canal, where she was taken over by David Hutcheson in 1851, and remained under Hutcheson and MacBrayne ownership until broken up in 1928. In 1875 she had a major rebuild, with the funnel moved forward of the paddles and small deck saloons added, as seen in this photo taken at Laggan Locks.

A bow view of *Glengarry* preparing to sail from Inverness.

Gondolier was built in 1866 for the service from Banavie to Fort Augustus and Inverness, the most northerly section of the Royal Route, and served this route until closing it in 1939, following which she was sold to the Admiralty for use as a blockship in Scapa Flow.

Gondolier on Loch Ness.

Another view of *Gondolier* on Loch Ness.

Cavalier was built in 1883 for the Glasgow to Inverness service, which she served until sold to the North Company in 1919.

Cavalier arriving at Oban.

Lochness had been built in 1853 for the Glasgow to Lochgoil service as *Lochgoil* and was later *Lough Foyle* based at Londonderry. MacBrayne purchased her in 1885 and she operated the Loch Ness service from Inverness to Fort Augustus until sold for scrapping in 1912. She is seen here in the Caledonian Canal.

Lochness at Foyers.

Lochness on Loch Ness.

Gairlochy was originally *Sultan* on the Clyde, built in 1861 for the Kilmun route. In the following year she was sold to Captain Alexander Williamson, and became part of his 'Turkish Fleet'. In 1891 she was sold to the Glasgow & South Western Railway and in 1893 to Captain John Williamson, who renamed her *Ardmore* before selling her to MacBrayne in 1894. He renamed her *Gairlochy*, shortened her by 30 ft, and fitted her with a canoe bow, to fit the Caledonian Canal locks. At the same time a deck saloon was added. She was placed on the Inverness to Banavie route opposite the *Gondolier*, leaving Inverness in the morning. She is seen here at speed on Loch Ness.

Above left: On 24 December 1919 *Gairlochy* was destroyed by fire at Fort Augustus. Parts of her can still be seen when the water level in the loch is low.

Above right: In 1912 the paddler *Lochness* was replaced by this *Lochness*. She was built in 1896 as *Clutha No.12* for the Clutha river service in Glasgow. When that ceased she was sold to become *Lough Neagh Queen* on Lough Neagh and became *Loch Leven Queen* in 1908 when she commenced a service from Ballachulish to Kinlochleven for workers involved in the building of the hydroelectric plant and aluminium smelter there. In 1911 she was taken over by MacBrayne and transferred to Loch Ness in the following year. She remained on the Loch Ness mail run until withdrawn in September 1928, after which road transport took the mails.

Chapter 6

RMS *Saint Columba* and *King George V*

On 3 October 1935 David MacBrayne Ltd purchased the two steamers *King George V* and *Queen Alexandra* of Turbine Steamers Ltd. The latter was rebuilt over the ensuing winter, when a third (dummy) funnel was added, her promenade deck extended aft and a promenade deck lounge installed. Renamed *Saint Columba*, she was a worthy successor to *Columba* on the Ardrishaig mail route, where she entered service for the summer 1936 season. She is seen here in pre-war condition with a good crowd aboard arriving at Dunoon.

A stern view of *Saint Columba* leaving Rothesay in pre-war condition with no wheelhouse. MacBrayne's had originally intended that she run from Oban to Fort William, but the cost of the necessary safety improvements proved prohibitive. Note the canvas over the stern rail, this was later replaced by a solid bulwark.

With the solid bulwarks aft, *Saint Columba* leaves Gourock in 1947 for the overnight berth at Greenock. Following her re-entry to service, she sailed from Gourock rather than from Glasgow and moored overnight at the Bristol Berth at Greenock as did *Lochfyne* until the withdrawal of the service in 1969.

Saint Columba, again with a good crowd on board, passing through the Kyles of Bute in 1936.

Saint Columba in the River Clyde at Glasgow off Harland & Wolff's Diesel engine works, being passed by *Kylemore*. This was probably taken on a Sunday when *Saint Columba* did not sail.

Geoffrey Grimshaw's classic shot of *Saint Columba* in post-war condition at speed off Buttock Point in the Kyles of Bute.

Saint Columba in Rothesay Bay on Coronation Day in 1953, showing the mainmast and wheelhouse added in 1947 when she was reconditioned after war service. By this time the cross-trees had been moved to the foremast.

King George V retained her name, and from 1936, operated the Staffa and Iona cruise from Oban, where she is seen here on her first day in service, in June 1936.

King George V storms past Rhuba nan Ghall lighthouse in 1936 en route from Tobermory to Staffa.

King George V in Loch Linnhe in 1952, the only year she had a vertical mainmast.

King George V at anchor off Staffa in 1954, with a small boat tendering to her.

King George V, with the wheelhouse and mainmast added in 1952, off Iona on Coronation Day, 3 June 1953. Note that the mainmast now has the same rake as the foremast.

King George V at Tobermory with an early British Railways container on the pier.

King George V in the north channel, Oban Bay.

King George V in lay up in the Queens Dock, Glasgow in the 1967-1968 winter.

The bell, builders' plate and original White Funnel engraved windows in the captain's cabin at the front of the promenade deck of *King George V.*

The main deck on *King George V*, a useful place to shelter from the rain and wind.

Chapter 7
Screw Steamers

The first *Clydesdale*, dating from 1862, ran on the Glasgow to Stornoway service. She is seen here at Kyle after 1893 when she received a new double-ended boiler and two funnels. She was lost by grounding in 1905.

Right: Fingal, seen here arriving at Rothesay, was built in 1896 for the Inverness to Fort Augustus service, but soon moved to the West Loch Tarbert to Islay routes. She later moved to the Oban to Bunessan service and was then used as a relief steamer, spending some time on the Glasgow to Loch Fyne cargo service. She was sold in 1917.

Below: A stern view of *Claymore* of 1881 leaving Kyle. She served on the Glasgow to Stornoway service.

Claymore at Lancefield Quay, Glasgow.

Claymore heading up the Clyde off Kilcreggan. She remained in service until 1931.

Above: Pelican was built in 1850 and was formerly owned by the City of Cork Steam Packet Co. She was purchased by David MacBrayne in 1888 for a proposed new service to Iceland. This did not materialise and she spent the rest of her days as a coal hulk at Portree and later Tobermory where she was wrecked in 1905.

Right: Staffa had been built in 1861 for service in Portugal and was purchased by MacBrayne in 1888 and served the route from Oban to the Outer Islands. She was sold for scrapping in 1908 and is seen here in lay up at Bowling.

Flowerdale at Oban. She was a former salvage vessel and operated the service from Oban to Castlebay and Lochboisdale from 1889 until lost in 1904.

Loch Aline was built in 1904 as *Plover* for MacBrayne and received the boiler and port engines of *Flowerdale*. She mainly operated the Outer Islands services from Oban, Mallaig and Kyle. In 1933 she was converted for use as the directors' yacht and was renamed *Loch Aline*. In May 1946 she was transferred to Burns & Laird Lines and laid up at Ardrossan until sold the following October for cargo use.

Above left: Loch Aline at Ardrossan with Burns & Laird's *Lairds Isle* in the background.

Above right: Loch Aline in lay-up at Ardrossan. Alongside her is the motor lighter *Iona*, built as the Thames lighter *C&B No.1* for Crosse & Blackwell in 1913 and purchased by MacBrayne in 1928 for use at Bowmore, Islay as a tender. Renamed *Lochgorm* in 1930, she was again renamed *Iona* in 1936 following the withdrawal of the paddle steamer of that name, in order to retain the name in the company.

Cygnet was built in 1904 as a sister to *Plover* and received the other engine and boiler from *Flowerdale*. She mainly served on the Outer Islands services and is seen her in Oban Bay.

Cygnet heading upriver. She was sold for scrapping in 1930 following the introduction of *Lochmor* and *Lochearn*.

The second *Clydesdale* was built in 1905. She was built for the Glasgow to Inverness service but moved to the Glasgow to Islay route after the loss of *Glendale* a few months later, and from 1920 onwards served the Glasgow to West Coast cargo runs in the winter months. She is seen here in the River Clyde at Glasgow passing Meadowside Granary.

Above: Clydesdale arriving at Oban. Note that by this time she had acquired a wheelhouse.

Right: A deck view of *Clydesdale* in her early years. She had a long life and was finally scrapped in 1953.

The last steamer to be built for David MacBrayne Ltd was *Lochness*, which came in 1929 for the Stornoway mail service. She is seen here in 1929 at Kyle in the short-lived grey hull period.

Lochness off Kyle. She served on the Stornoway route until December 1947 when she was replaced by *Loch Seaforth*, and was sold in 1955 to Greek owners, for whom she sailed as *Myrtidiotissa* until scrapped in 1974.

T.S.S. LOCHNESS at Castlebay, Barra.

A view of *Lochness* at Castlebay, Barra, from the 1951 timetable. In 1948 and 1949 she operated the Inner Islands service from Oban to Castlebay and Lochboisdale via Coll and Tiree whilst *Lochearn* and *Lochmor* were away being re-engined.

1. A deck view on *Columba*, entitled *On the Clyde*, showing the gentry enjoying themselves on deck en route to their Highland Shooting Lodges. The route to Oban via Ardrishaig and the Crinan Canal was know as The Royal Route from its having been used by Queen Victoria on her visit to Scotland in 1847. She was sent that way reportedly by the glowing account she had of it from the Grand Duke Constantine, who, on a visit to Scotland the year before, had been sent that way by the Admiralty.

2. C.L.D. Duckworth is commemorated with a window in Christ Church, East Sheen, Greater London, including a stained glass image of *Columba*.

3. The figurehead of the 1881 *Claymore*, now in display in the Scottish Maritime Museum at Irvine.

4. *Hebrides* in the Albert Harbour, Greenock, when she was laid up there between her withdrawal in June 1955 with the advent of *Loch Ard*, and her sale for scrapping in August of that year.

5. Another view of *Hebrides* in the Albert Harbour.

6. *Saint Columba* arriving at Tarbert.

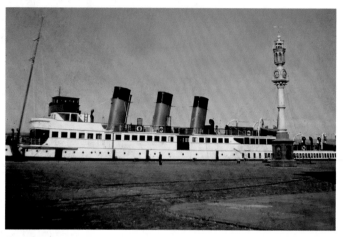

7. *Saint Columba* at Greenock Custom House Quay, her overnight lay-up berth. She was the only three-funnelled British coastal excursion steamer. The third funnel was a dummy, used for storing deck chairs.

8. *Saint Columba* being fuelled at her overnight berth at Greenock. Note the milk churns.

9. The five-funnelled steamer! *Saint Columba* and *King George V* lying alongside each other in winter lay-up at Greenock's Albert Harbour.

10. *King George V* in May 1956 on a charter to Collins the publishers at Bridge Wharf, Glasgow.

11. *King George V* arriving at Oban.

12. *King George V* at the Railway Pier, Oban.

13. The builder's plate and bell of *King George V*.

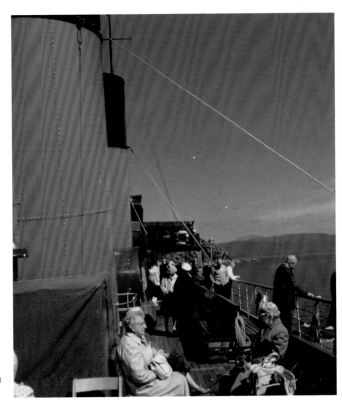

14. *Right:* A deck shot on *King George V* in 1971.

15. *Below:* *King George V* anchored off Iona, 1969, with a red boat tendering to her.

16. A long queue of passengers waits to be ferried out to *King George V* at Iona in the early fifties.

17. *King George V*, with *Lochnevis* and *Lochbroom* alongside in winter-lay up at Greenock in the early fifties.

18. *King George V* in winter lay-up in Queens Dock, Glasgow in early 1968.

19. *King George V* in Lamont's dry dock at Greenock.

20. A stern view of the previous image. Note the loose propeller on the floor of the dry dock below the stern.

21. *Loch Frisa* and *Saint Columba* at Greenock Custom House Quay.

22. *Loch Carron* in Kingston Dock, Glasgow, with the former yacht *Taransay*, which ran briefly from Glasgow to Campbeltown in 1948, across the end of the dock.

23. The bow of *Lochinvar* in dry dock.

24. *Lochfyne* arriving at Dunoon in summer 1969, on her return form Ardrishaig ...

25. ... and berthed at Dunoon on the same occasion.

26. *Lochfyne* berthed at Tarbert pier in the 1960s.

27. *Lochnevis c.1960* at Fort William with a fleet of MacBrayne buses awaiting her arrival. These buses would have gone to Inverness or back to Oban both direct and via Glencoe and Tyndrum.

28. *Lochnevis* outward bound for Tarbert and Ardrishaig, during a period when she was relieving *Lochfyne*, at Dunoon, from the promenade deck of the pier.

29. *Lochnevis* at Oban Railway Pier in September 1969. Note the railway carriages in the background.

30. *Lochnevis* at
Tobermory with
Lochbroom and a puffer
alongside her.

31. *Lochiel* in
winter lay-up in the
James Watt Dock,
Greenock.

32. *Lochiel* in West Loch Tarbert.

33. *Loch Seaforth* undergoing winter overhaul in Victoria Harbour, Greenock with repairs having been done to her bow. Behind her is a New Zealand Shipping Co. cargo ship.

34. *Loch Seaforth* departs Mallaig in 1968.

35. Heading for Kyle and Stornoway.

36. The wreck of *Loch Seaforth* at Tiree in 1973, after having been raised form Gunna Sound, towed to Tiree pier and again sinking. The floating crane, *Ulrich Harms*, is raising her at the pier.

37. The launch of *Claymore* into the River Leven at the Denny yard at Dumbarton on 14 March 1955.

38. *Claymore*, looking magnificent in this shot, which shows the Highlander emblem on the bow well, carrying on the image from the figurehead of the old *Claymore*.

39. *Claymore* at her regular berth at the Railway Pier, Oban.

40. *Claymore* departing the Railway Pier, Oban.

41. *Claymore* laid up in the East India Harbour, Greenock, in summer 1975, lying behind *Maid of Cumbrae*, with *Loch Carron* at the river berth.

42. *Claymore* departing from Tobermory.

43. *Claymore* loading a car at Tiree, 1975.

44. Sheep being unloaded on the hoof from *Claymore* at Tiree on the same occasion.

45. Passengers arriving at Tiree on the same day, led by a pipe band.

46. *Lochnell* at the steps at the end of the Railway Pier at Oban, from where she operated to Lismore.

47. *Lochbuie* arriving at Tobermory with her short-lived blue hull, used from 1960 to 1962.

48. *Loch Toscaig* arriving at Kyle, again with a blue hull.

49. *Loch Toscaig* at Oban North Pier in 1969 at which time she was on the Lismore run. Note the MacBrayne bus in the background.

50. *Loch Arkaig* at Mallaig shortly after entering service. Occasionally a car would be carried for Raasay on the landing platform.

51. *Loch Arkaig* at Mallaig with the car ferry *Clansman* behind her, 1973.

52. Remarkably, MacBrayne's pioneer motor vessel *Comet* of 1907 survives, in use as a houseboat at Shoreham where she has lain for the past sixty-three years.

53. The 'red boats' were a feature of Iona for generations, ferrying passengers to and from *King George V* and her predecessors on the route. Here is *Iona* in 1969.

54. And *Lochshiel* moored at the jetty at Iona on the same occasion. She had operated on the service on Loch Shiel from Glenfinnan to Acharacle from her building in 1953 until transferred to Iona ten years later.

55. The Red Boat *Eigg* served the same function at Eigg, one of the Small Isles.

56. *Left:* She was the main means of getting cargo to the island. Here a load of planks is being unloaded from *Loch Arkaig* on to her in 1973.

57. *Above:* Cargo was handed this way at Rum, Eigg and Muck until the last few years when piers were built.

58. The MacBrayne ticket office window at Rothesay.

59. A horse being unloaded from *Claymore* at Tiree.

60. A dog takes the ropes of *Claymore* at Castlebay.

61. The Art Deco pier building at Port Ellen.

62. Port Askaig in the days before the car ferry.

63. The MacBrayne bus station at Killermont Street, Glasgow.

64. The red ensign and MacBrayne pennant flying from *Lochinvar*.

65. *Above left:* In the latter part of the nineteenth century, MacBrayne's issued hard-backed guide books with timetables bound in at the end. This is an issue from 1884.

66. *Above right:* The early guidebooks had this map, known as the Balloon Map bound into the front of them.

67. *Above left:* By the 1890s the guidebooks had adopted a red cover to match the steamers' funnels, as in this example from 1898, which had photographic illustrations rather than the engravings of the earlier issues.

68. *Above right:* By the early 1900s a card-covered guidebook was available, as in this one from 1904 with a picture of *Columba* on the front cover.

69. *Above left:* The back of this guidebook featured a faked image of *Columba* framed by Fingal's Cave.

70. *Above right:* By the 1930s the timetable was in a 6 in x 8.5 in booklet format, with the cover changing each year. This is the issue for 1935 with *Lochfyne* and an early bus on the cover. This was an eighty-page publication, with much space given to circular tours.

71. The centenary timetable of 1951 was a 7.5 in x 5 in landscape-format timetable, with three articles, Glasgow to Inverness, Oban to Staffa and Iona and The Inner Islands, the Outer Islands, the Isles of Lewis and Skye preceding the timetable section.

72. The rear cover of the 1951 timetable showed *Lochfyne* and a MacBrayne bus. 1952 and 1953 had a similar format, with a much smaller text section in the front of only two or three pages.

73. *Above left:* By 1956 the timetable was in a fold-open brochure format. This continued for the next five years.

74. *Middle:* In 1962, the same format was used, but this year there were colour illustrations inside.

75. *Above right:* 1963 and 1964 saw an extra large format of 13.25 in x 9.75 in. A series of combined coach and steamer tours were introduced, whilst 1964 saw the first car ferry services.

76. *Above left:* 1965 to 1970 saw this image of flags on the timetable covers. 1965 was the same size as 1964, 1966 was smaller at 10 in x 8.5 in, and this continued until 1969 for a separate Inclusive Tours brochure, while 1967 to 1970 were in a small format of 5.5 in x 4 in, as seen here in the 1967 cover

77. *Above right:* 1971 and 1972, under the aegis of the Scottish Transport Group, saw an 8.75 in x 5.5 in publication, with plain pages and no illustrations inside, apart from those inside the cover.

78. From 1966 to 1970 MacBrayne issued small folders for local services in different areas. Illustrated are, clockwise from left, those for The Clyde, Oban, Skye and the Outer Islands. Also available were issues for Islay, Mull, Fort William, Inverness and Mallaig and Kyle of Lochalsh.

79. *Right:* A linear
route map dating
from the 1960s
from Gourock to
Ardrishaig, with
a drawing of
Lochfyne on the
cover, although
Saint Columba
is illustrated on
the map inside.
The reverse shows
the MacBrayne
bus route from
Ardrishaig to
Glasgow.

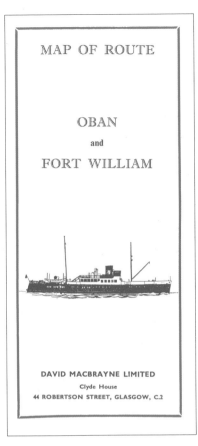

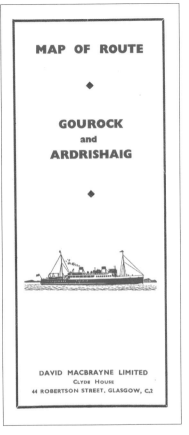

80. *Above right:* A similar route map from Oban to Fort William with *Lochnevis* illustrated in the cover. The reverse shows the bus route from Fort William to Inverness. A third version of this showed the bus routes from Glasgow to Fort William and Fort William to Inverness, the former showing a MacBrayne cargo vessel in the Clyde and *Lochfyne* at Fort William.

81. A railway-style luggage label used by MacBrayne.

82. A MacBrayne letter-heading from the early years of the twentieth century.

83. A selection of MacBrayne tickets:

Top row from left: Rothesay and Gourock; exchange for Wemyss Bay ticket; Tarbert or Ardrishaig to Glasgow (Bridge Wharf); Juvenile Organisation ticket, dating from prior to 1939.

Second row from left: Colintraive or Tighnabruaich to Dunoon or Innellan; Fort William to Staffa and Iona and back Child ticket.

Third row from left: Oban to Craignure; Oban Games day return on Oban exc'n steamer; Islay or Jura and Gigha to Tarbert, in charge of livestock.

Fourth row from left: Stornoway to Mallaig; Motor Cycle Single; Kyle to Outer Island and back; Outer Hebrides Tour.

84. This splendid artist's impression from a MacBrayne publicity leaflet, presenting the first MacBrayne car ferries prior to their introduction in 1964, is a fitting end to this volume. The introduction to the Uig triangle (Skye-Harris-North Uist) in April 1964 of MV Hebrides marked the beginning of the end of David MacBrayne Ltd, who were finally merged into Caledonian MacBrayne in January 1973, less than nine years after their introduction.

Lochbroom had been built in 1871 for the Aberdeen Steam Navigation Co. as *City of London* and was purchased in 1931 to replace *Claymore* on the Glasgow to Lochinver service, which operated every ten days. She is seen here at Ardrossan and was broken up in 1937.

Lochgarry, seen here on trials, was transferred from Burns & Laird Lines in 1937. She had been built in 1898 as *Vulture* for the Burns fleet and renamed *Lairdsrock* when they merged with Laird in 1929. She replaced *Lochbroom* on the West Highland cruises from Glasgow.

Lochgarry off Fort William. She lasted in the fleet only a short while, being requisitioned for naval service in 1940 and sinking off Rathlin on 21 January 1942 whilst in use as a transport from Scotland to Iceland.

In 1946 and 1947 the small screw steamer *Robina* was chartered. She had been built in 1914 for excursion service at Morecambe and had served from 1925 until the outbreak of war as a tender-cum-excursion vessel at Belfast. She spent the war years as a tender on the Clyde. She spent 1946 offering excursions at Oban and 1947 on the Glasgow to Lochgoilhead service, in which year she is seen off Gourock.

Robina off Gourock in 1947. In 1948 she was sold to Southampton operator Red Funnel and was scrapped in 1955.

In November 1947 MacBrayne took over McCallum, Orme & Co. Ltd with their steamers
Dunara Castle and *Hebrides*. *Dunara Castle*, seen here at Lancefield Quay, had been built in
1875 for Martin Orme & Co., and made her final sailing in January 1948. She was noted for
her role in evacuating the inhabitants of St Kilda in 1930 and regularly called there.

Hebrides had been built in 1898 for John McCallum & Co.'s service from Glasgow to the West
Highlands. They merged with Orme in 1929, and she continued on this service until withdrawal
in 1952, in her final years carrying cargo only. She is seen here off Greenock.

Above: Hebrides on the slip at Blackwood & Gordon's yard at Port Glasgow.

Left: Hebrides dressed overall at her Glasgow terminus of Kingston Dock on MacBrayne centenary day, 10 February 1951.

Above: Hebrides lying with *Lochgorm* outside her, loading cargo at Oban North Pier.

Right: Hebrides lying alongside *Lochgorm* in the river at Glasgow at *Waverley*'s present berth.

Chapter 8
Cargo Vessels

Handa, seen here leaving the North Pier, Oban, had been built in 1876 as *Aros Castle* for Martin Orme and purchased by David MacBrayne in 1887. She operated on various routes, latterly on the cargo run from Glasgow to Oban, Mull and Loch Sunart via the Crinan Canal. She was known as 'MacBrayne's Gladstone Bag' on account of her large cargo capacity in comparison to her size.

Texa was built in 1884 as *James Mutter* and ran to Islay. In 1889 she was purchased by MacBrayne and worked on various cargo services from Glasgow, latterly that to Loch Fyne. She was sold in 1917.

At some stage in her career, *Texa* had the derrick removed from her foremast and a stand-alone crane fitted further aft. She is seen here heading up the River Clyde between Erskine and Langbank.

Brenda was built in 1894, and had second-hand engines from a yacht. She served the cargo routes from Glasgow to Oban and Mull and to Inverness via the Crinan Canal, and is seen here off Fort William. She was sold for breaking up in 1929.

Lochshiel was a motor vessel built in 1929 to replace *Brenda,* although the service now ran via the Mull of Kintyre. She is seen here at Glasgow off Anderston. She was the first vessel ordered by David MacBrayne (1928) Ltd.

Lochshiel berthed at Glasgow. She served in the fleet until 1952.

Lochshiel lying forward of *Claymore* at Lancefield Quay, Glasgow, with the General terminus mooring buoy clearly visible.

Lochshiel with *Lochdunvegan* at Lancefield Quay, Glasgow.

Lochdunvegan had been built in 1891 for G.&J. Burns as *Grouse*, later coming under the Coast Lines flag as *Denbigh Coast*. She was transferred to the new MacBrayne company in 1929 and ran mainly on the weekly Glasgow to Stornoway service, calling only at Tobermory and Portree. She was sold for breaking up in 1948. She is seen here off Partick.

Lochdunvegan in the Sound of Mull.

Lochgorm had been built in 1896 as *Lily* for Laird Line, and had latterly been Burns & Laird Lines' *Lairdspool*. She was transferred to MacBrayne's in 1937 and ran on the Glasgow to Stornoway run. She was sold for scrapping in 1951 and is seen here in Kingston Dock.

Lochgorm in Albert Dock, Greenock.

In addition to *Hebrides* and *Dunara Castle*, the cargo steamer *Challenger* was taken over from McCallum Orme, She had been built in 1897 and taken over by Jack Bros in 1929. This company was taken over by McCallum Orme in 1935. Jack Bros ran a cargo service from Kingston Dock, Glasgow, where she is seen here, to a number of small ports in the Western Isles. She was scrapped in 1948.

Lochbroom was built as a coastal patrol vessel during the Second World War but was uncompleted at the end of the war. She was named *Empire Maysong* and was purchased by MacBrayne in 1949 for the Glasgow to Stornoway service. She served on the MacBrayne cargo routes until sold in 1971 and is seen here on trials.

Lochbroom at Tobermory.

Loch Frisa, seen here off Dalmuir, was a standard, Canadian-built steam coaster dating from 1946. She came into the MacBrayne fleet in 1949. She ran on the cargo services from Glasgow to the Hebrides and was sold to Greek owners in 1963. She was the last steamer to be purchased by the company.

Loch Frisa berthed in Glasgow. Note the different position of the name at the bow. It is probable that this was a temporary name applied when she was purchased. The purchase took place in Amsterdam and a MacBrayne captain brought her back from there.

In 1953 the motor vessel *Örnen* was purchased from Swedish owners and renamed *Lochdunvegan*. She replaced *Lochgorm* on the Glasgow to Stornoway cargo service and served the company until sold in 1973.

Lochdunvegan in the River Clyde off Erskine Hospital, now Mar Hall hotel. In 1973 she served as a supplementary car ferry from Oban to Tiree.

Loch Carron, seen here off Erskine, was built for the company in 1951 and ran on the Outer Island cargo service from Glasgow.

The new *Loch Carron* in Oban Bay in 1951 with *Lochnell*.

In 1953 *Loch Carron* had her mainmast lengthened, as seen in this illustration, to carry the masthead light at a sufficient height to meet new regulations. She was the last cargo steamer in the fleet and was sold in 1977 by which time all the cargo was being taken by road and car ferry.

Loch Ard was built in 1955 to replace *Hebrides* on the Outer Islands cargo service. She is seen here at her Glasgow berth in Kingston Dock. From 1964 she was on the Islay cargo service, but when the car ferry took over the route from West Loch Tarbert in 1970 she was redundant and was sold the following year to Greek owners.

Chapter 9
Motor Vessels

MacBrayne was an early pioneer of the internal combustion engine, the first such vessel in the fleet being *Comet*, acquired in 1907 and previously operating on the Thames for a couple of years as a motor yacht. She initially served the Ballachulish to Kinlochleven service and later moved to the Greenock (Princes Pier) and Gourock to Lochgoilhead service. She is seen here off Gourock. Early in her career she was also used to assist *Linnet* on the Crinan Canal in the peak season. She was withdrawn in 1946 and sold the following year for use at Shoreham where she survives as a houseboat.

Right: A second motor vessel, named *Scout* was built in 1907 at Troon for the Ballachulish to Kinlochleven service. She is seen here at the berth adjacent to the slate quarries at Ballachulish.

Below: These early motor vessels were fuelled by paraffin, which contributed to the destruction of *Scout* following an engine blow back on 19 August 1913.

A third, larger, motor vessel, *Lochinvar*, was built in 1908 for the Oban to Tobermory mail service. She is seen here early in her career fitted with a single tall steamer-type funnel.

Lochinvar in her original condition. Like the other early motorships, she was originally paraffin-fuelled.

Later, possibly after her re-engining in 1926, a single exhaust pipe was fitted for each of *Lochinvar*'s three engines.

Right: Lochinvar in Lamont's dry dock at
Greenock. In early 1933 a conventional funnel
was fitted, shorter than the original. At this time
a large crane was fitted amidships, as can be seen
here.

Below: A well-filled *Lochinvar* at Oban North
Pier prior to her 1949 rebuild with *Hebrides*, with
Lochearn inboard of her, moored aft.

Lochinvar inbound off Dunollie prior to 1949 with the motorship funnel and no wheelhouse.

Lochinvar at Tobermory prior to 1949.

Right: Lochinvar during her 1949 rebuild at Lamont's dry dock, Greenock. At this time she received new engines, new decks, an observation shelter and a wheelhouse and was reduced from triple screw to twin screw. Note the funnels of *King George V* in winter lay up in the background.

Below: Another view of *Lochinvar* in dry dock in 1949. At that time she had much of her hull plating replaced, as can be seen from the grey patches on the hull.

Lochinvar between her 1949 rebuild and 1952 when a mainmast was fitted. She was withdrawn in 1960 was sold for a service between Sheerness and Southend on the Thames Estuary under the name *Anzio I*. She was again sold in 1966 for use at Cromarty, but was wrecked on her delivery voyage with the loss of all her crew.

Following the purchase by Coast Lines and the LMSR in 1928, two motorships were ordered from Ardrossan Dockyard for the Outer Isles services from Oban and Mallaig. Here we see the launch of *Lochearn*, the first of these, on 29 April 1930.

Lochearn on trials in the short-lived grey hull livery applied in 1930.

Lochearn at Oban. She operated the service from Oban to Tobermory, Coll, Tiree, Castlebay (Barra) and Lochboisdale (South Uist).

Lochearn, in a postcard view, arriving at Gott, Tiree, on her regular run from Oban to Castlebay and Lochboisdale. She was withdrawn in 1964 and sold to Greek owners for whom she saw little or no service.

The launch of *Lochmor* at Ardrossan on 15 May 1930.

Right: Lochmor arriving at Mallaig in grey-hulled condition in 1930.

Below: Lochmor in the Sound of Mull after the funnel was shortened. Her route ran from Mallaig to Armadale, Kylerhea, Kyle, Raasay, Portree, Tarbert (Harris), Rodel, Lochmaddy, Lochboisdale, Canna, Rhum, Eigg and back to Mallaig. She too, was sold in 1964 to Greece. Prior to 1939 calls were also made on some sailings at Stockinish in Harris, and at Dunvegan between Lochmaddy and Lochboisdale.

Lochfyne was built in 1931 with what was, for that era, a revolutionary diesel-electric propulsion system. She operated in the summer months out of Oban and was on the winter Tarbert and Ardrishaig servicet. From 1959, after the withdrawal of *Saint Columba* she was on the Ardrishaig service year round, although the winter service only ran to Tarbert from 1960 onwards. She is seen here at Tarbert, Loch Fyne.

Lochfyne off Gourock. Initially, until the advent of *King George V* in 1936, she was on the Staffa and Iona run from Oban in the summer months, and from then on mainly served Fort William and, from 1947, excursions such as that to the Six Lochs and to Tobermory and Loch Sunart from Oban.

Lochfyne entering Ardrishaig harbour., early in her career without a mainmast.

Another view of *Lochfyne* approaching Ardrishaig in 1967.

Lochfyne arriving off Rothesay.

Lochfyne northbound in Loch Linnhe, approaching the Corran Narrows.

Right: Lochfyne in Lamont's dry dock at Greenock. She continued on the Ardrishaig service until autumn 1969, and was sold the following year and, after service as a floating power station in the Gareloch, was finally scrapped at Dalmuir in 1974.

Below: Lochnevis was a smaller single-funnelled version of *Lochfyne*. She entered service in 1934 and indirectly replaced *Glencoe* on the Malling-Kyle-Portree mail service. She is seen here on trials off Innellan.

Above: Lochnevis off Mallaig.

Left: In pre-war summers *Lochnevis* also ran excursions from Portree to Gairloch where she is seen here, and Loch Torridon, and from Mallaig to Loch Scavaig.

Lochnevis had occasional spells as a relief vessel on the Ardrishaig mail service, and is seen here at Tarbert with a Christmas tree at the masthead.

From 1959 *Lochnevis* replaced *Lochfyne* on the Oban excursion roster, including the Fort William sailings. She also spent spells relieving *Lochiel* on the Islay mail service, as when she was photographed here at West Loch Tarbert. In 1965 she was on the Islay mail run whilst *Lochiel* operated a car ferry service.

Lochnevis at Port Askaig. Note the MacBrayne buses on the pier. Services were operated to Bowmore and Port Ellen and to Portnahaven in the south-west of the island.

Lochnevis unloading an Austin A35 van at Colonsay, which was served at that time as part of the Islay service with two sailings a week in summer and one in winter. She was sold to Dutch owners in 1970 and was broken up four years later.

Lochiel was built in 1939 to replace *Pioneer* on the Islay mail service. She was similar to *Lochnevis*, although having diesel rather than diesel-electric machinery. She originally operated from Oban to Fort William until November 1940 because a necessary extension to West Loch Tarbert pier, where she is seen here, was not complete.

Lochiel passing Greenock, probably on her way back from overhaul. She remained in service until replaced by the car ferry *Arran* in 1970, and was then sold to Norwest Shipping for a service from Fleetwood to the Isle of Man under the name *Norwest Laird* which only lasted for one season, and then became a floating pub at Bristol until broken up in situ in 1995.

Loch Seaforth was built in 1947 for the Mallaig and Kyle to Stornoway service to replace *Lochness*. She is seen here on trials.

Loch Seaforth at Kyle of Lochalsh with *Lochnevis* across the end of the pier in her original condition. She served the Stornoway route until January 1972 when she was replaced by *Iona*, shortly after which the mainland port was moved to Ullapool. Loch Seaforth went to the Oban-Lochboisdale service, and ran aground in the Sound of Gunna between Coll and Tiree on 22 March 1973. She was towed to Tiree pier where she sank, and was later towed to Troon for scrapping.

Claymore was the final large motor vessel to be built for MacBrayne prior to the introduction of the car ferry. She was built in 1955 to replace *Lochearn* on the Oban -Lochboisdale service, and is seen here off Erskine following a 'show the flag' event in Kingston Dock.

Claymore at Oban Railway Pier, with *Lochnevis* moored outside her.

Claymore at Tobermory.

Claymore approaching Gott Pier.

Claymore at Castlebay, Barra with various vehicles on the pier to collect cargo from her.

Claymore at Lochboisdale, South Uist. She served the route until 1976 when she was sold to Greek owners, rebuilt and employed on the one-day cruise trade from Piraeus to the Saronic Islands for a number of years as *City of Hydra*.

SHIP
FOR
INNER ISLANDS MAIL
AFTERNOON CRUISE
COLONSAY 12
PASSENGERS EMBARK
11.45

Claymore's fan-board on the occasion of her first visit to Colonsay in 1965, when she offered day cruises from Oban to Colonsay, Tobermory and Fort William (non-landing).

Claymore at Oban Railway Pier in 1956.

Chapter 10
Smaller Vessels

Linnet was built in 1866 to supply the link in the Royal Route between *Iona*, and later *Columba*, at Ardrishaig and *Chevalier* at Crinan through the Crinan Canal. She is seen here in her original condition prior to 1894 when she received a bridge aft of the funnel and a small deckhouse. She replaced horse-drawn track boats, and lasted in service until 1929 and was sold for use as a club house at Shandon on the Gareloch. This was wrecked in a storm in 1932.

Above: Linnet in original condition with tall funnel behind the houses in Ardrishaig.

Right: Mabel was built in 1883 for use on Loch Maree and was purchased by David MacBrayne four years later.

Mabel was withdrawn after the 1911 summer season and was laid up for many years near the Loch Maree Hotel, where she is seen here.

The first *Lochbuie* was built in Alkmaar in The Netherlands for the company in 1937, and offered cruises from Fort William. She was requisitioned in 1939 and served as a hospital launch of the Clyde during the war years. In 1947 she was sold for use as a yacht.

In 1947 the hospital launch *Galen* was purchased and renamed *Lochnell* for the service from Oban to Lismore. In 1965 she moved to the Kyle to Toscaig service and in 1968 to Tobermory to Mingary. She was withdrawn in 1981 and is seen here in her original condition. Note the huge house flag.

Lochnell approaching the steps at Oban from where the Lismore service ran. She can still be seen about the Clyde in private use.

The second *Lochbuie* was a former RAF rescue pinnace and was purchased in 1949 for use on the Tobermory to Mingary route which she served until 1965, ending her days with a further three years on the Lismore service. She is seen here in Tobermory Bay.

Lochbuie, again in Tobermory Bay, spent most of her career in a black hull, but spent a period with a light blue hull *c.*1960.

Loch Toscaig was a motor fishing vessel purchased in 1955 for the service from Kyle of Lochalsh to Toscaig, for Applecross. From 1964 she was on the Lismore service from Oban, where she is seen here. She was sold in 1973 and later offered fishing trips from Gourock.

Loch Arkaig was a former coastal minesweeper and was purchased in 1959 and rebuilt for the Portree mail service from Mallaig and Kyle. From 1964 she also ran to the Small Isles of Eigg, Rum and Canna. She is seen here at Mallaig with the car ferry *Clansman*. She sank in Mallaig Harbour in 1969 and was later sold for use in Spain, where she sank near Cadiz whilst undergoing trials in 1985.

At many of the present car ferry ports, passengers and cargo were transferred to and from the mail steamer by small open boats prior to the building of piers. Here we see two such craft lashed together at Craignure, where the pier was opened in 1964.

The ferry boat at Coll in the final days of such service there before the pier was opened in 1963.

Chapter 11
A MacBrayne Miscellany

Blackmillbay Pier on Luing, taken from the 1910 *Mountaineer* and showing a cow about to be loaded.

The making of the film *The Maggie* in the river Clyde at Glasgow in 1953, with a puffer named *Maggie* for the film. The puffers *Boer* and *Inca* were used in the making the film. To the right is what may be the stern of MacBrayne's *Hebrides*.

MURRAYS' SCOTTISH TOURIST ADVERTISER.   137

GLASGOW AND THE HIGHLANDS.

(*Royal Route* via *Crinan and Caledonian Canals.*)

THE ROYAL MAIL STEAMERS—

IONA,	CHEVALIER,	GONDOLIER,	STAFFA,
MOUNTAINEER,	PIONEER,	EDINBURGH,	LINNET,
CLANSMAN,	CLYDESDALE,	CYGNET,	PLOVER,

DOLPHIN, MARY JANE, and INVERARAY CASTLE,

Sail during the Season for Oban, Fort-William, Inverness, Staffa, Iona, Glencoe, Tobermory, Portree, Gairloch, Ullapool, Lochinver and Stornoway, affording Tourists an opportunity of Visiting the Magnificent Scenery of Glencoe, the Coolin Hills, Loch Coruisk, Loch Maree, and the famed Islands of Staffa and Iona.

⁎ These Vessels afford in their passage a view of the beautiful Scenery of the Clyde, with all its Watering-places—the Island and Kyles of Bute—Island of Arran—Mountains of Cowal, Knapdale, and Kintyre —Lochfyne—Crinan—with the Islands of Jura, Scarba, Mull, and many others of the Western Sea—the Whirlpool of Corryvreckan—the Mountains of Lorn, of Morven, of Appin, of Kingairloch, and Ben Nevis— Inverlochy—the Lands of Lochiel, the scene of the wanderings of Prince Charles, and near to where the Clans raised his Standard in the '45— Lochaber—the Caledonian Canal—Loch Lochy—Loch Oich—Loch Ness, with the Glens and Mountains on either side, and the celebrated FALLS OF FOYERS.   Books descriptive of the Route may be had on board the Steamers.

Time-Bills, with Maps, sent post free on application to the Proprietors, DAVID HUTCHESON & CO., 119 Hope Street, Glasgow.

Glasgow, 1868.

Hutcheson's, and later MacBrayne's, advertised their sailings in Scottish guidebooks. This is an early example of such, from 1868.

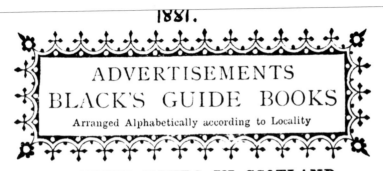

SUMMER TOURS IN SCOTLAND.
GLASGOW AND THE HIGHLANDS
(*Royal Route* via *Crinan and Caledonian Canals.*)
Special Tourist Cabin Tickets issued during the Season,
For One Week, £3 ; or Two Weeks, £5.

Giving the *privilege* of the run of *all the undernamed Steamers to any part of the Highlands* where they may call at during the time specified.
Breakfast, Dinner, and Tea for One Week, £2 additional.

THE ROYAL			MAIL STEAMERS

CLAYMORE (New Screw Steamship)

COLUMBA	ISLAY	GLENCOE	INVERARAY CASTLE
IONA	CHEVALIER	GONDOLIER	STAFFA	FINGAL
MOUNTAINEER	PIONEER	GLENGARRY	LINNET	LOCHIEL
CLANSMAN	CLYDESDALE	CYGNET	PLOVER	LOCHAWE

AND QUEEN OF THE LAKE.

Sail during the season for Port Ellen, Port Askaig, Islay, Oban, Fort-William, Inverness, Staffa, Iona, Glencoe, Loch Awe, Tobermory, Portree, Strome Ferry, Gairloch, Ullapool, Lochinver, Lochmaddy, Tarbert, Harris, and Stornoway ; affording Tourists an opportunity of visiting the Magnificent Scenery of Loch Awe, Glencoe, the Coolin Hills, Loch Coruisk, Loch Maree, and the famed Islands of Staffa and Iona.

*** These vessels afford in their passage a view of the beautiful scenery of the Clyde, with all its Watering-Places—the Island and Kyles of Bute—Island of Arran—Mountains of Cowal, Knapdale, and Kintyre—Lochfyne—Crinan—with the Islands of Jura, Scarba, Mull, and many others of the Western Sea—The Whirlpool of Corryvreckan—the Mountains of Lorn, of Morven, of Appin, of Kingairloch, and Ben Nevis—Inverlochy—The Lands of Lochiel, the scene of the wanderings of Prince Charles, and near to where the clans raised his Standard in the '45—Lochaber—the Caledonian Canal—Loch Lochy—Loch Oich—Loch Ness, with the Glens and Mountains on either side, and the celebrated FALLS OF FOYERS. From Ardrishaig to Ford, the route passes through the picturesque valley of Kilmartin and by Kilmartin Castle, Carnassery Castle, Bull's Pass, Dog's Head Loch, and Ederline Loch. The attractions on Loch Awe are numerous. There are twenty-four Islands, many of them richly wooded, and crowned by the ruins of four Castles and two Monasteries. At the foot of the Lake is the romantic Pass of Brander, where MacDougall of Lorne encountered the Bruce, and where Ben Cruachan rises 3800 feet from the Awe. Books descriptive of the route may be had on board the Steamers. Official Guide Book, 2d. ; Illustrated, 6d. ; Cloth, 1s.

Time-Bill, with Map and Tourist Fares, sent post free on application to the Proprietor, DAVID MACBRAYNE, 119 Hope Street, Glasgow.

GLASGOW, 1881.

A

A similar advertisement, by now for MacBrayne, from Black's *Guide book to Scotland* in 1881, by this time showing a drawing of *Columba*.

SUMMER TOURS IN SCOTLAND.

1885.

THE

ROYAL ROUTE.

GLASGOW AND THE HIGHLANDS.

Via CRINAN and CALEDONIAN CANALS.

TOURISTS' SPECIAL CABIN TICKETS issued during the Season, giving the privilege of the run of all the undernamed Steamers, to any part of the Highlands at which they may call during the time specified.

For One Week, £3; Two Weeks, £5; or Six Separate Days, £3, 10s.

NEW ROYAL MAIL STEAM SHIP "GRENADIER."

COLUMBA.	MOUNTAINEER.	CLAYMORE.	LOCHIEL.
IONA.	PIONEER.	CLANSMAN.	FINGAL.
CHEVALIER.	LOCHAWE.	CLYDESDALE.	ISLAY.
GONDOLIER.	GLENCOE.	CAVALIER.	LOCHNESS.
GLENGARRY.	LINNET.	STAFFA.	INVERARAY CASTLE.

THE ROYAL MAIL SWIFT PASSENGER STEAMER

"COLUMBA" or "IONA,"

Sails daily from MAY till OCTOBER, from GLASGOW at 7 A.M., and from GREENOCK about 9 A.M., in connection with Express Trains from London and the South, Edinburgh and Glasgow, &c., for *KYLES OF BUTE, TARBERT,* and *ARDRISHAIG,* conveying Passengers for *OBAN, GLENCOE, INVERNESS, LOCHAWE, STAFFA* and *IONA, MULL, SKYE, GAIRLOCH, STORNOWAY, &c., &c.*

A WHOLE DAY'S SAIL BY THE "COLUMBA" OR "IONA,"

From GLASGOW to ARDRISHAIG and Back (180 miles).

CABIN FARE,	.	.	6s.	or including Breakfast, Dinner, and Tea,	.	.	12s.
FORE CABIN FARE,	.	.	3s. 6d.	do., do., do., do.	.	.	7s.

A WEEK'S TOUR TO STORNOWAY,

BY STEAM SHIP

"CLAYMORE" OR "CLANSMAN,"

Via MULL OF KINTYRE, going and returning through the SOUNDS OF JURA, MULL, and SKYE, calling at OBAN, TOBERMORY, PORTREE, and intermediate places.

CABIN FARE with Superior Sleeping Accommodation, **45s.**; or, including Meals, **80s.** The Route is through scenery rich in historical interest, and unequalled for grandeur and variety. These vessels leave Glasgow every Monday and Thursday about 12 noon, and Greenock about 5 p.m., returning from Stornoway every Monday and Wednesday.

The Steam Ship **CAVALIER** or **STAFFA** will leave Glasgow every Monday and Thursday at 11 a.m., and Greenock at 4 p.m., for Inverness and Back (via Mull of Kintyre) leaving Inverness every Monday and Thursday morning; Cabin Fare for the Trip, with First-class Sleeping Accommodation, **30s.**; or including Meals, by Steamer leaving Glasgow on Mondays, **56s.**; on Thursday, **60s.**

OFFICIAL GUIDE BOOK, 3d.; ILLUSTRATED, 6d.; Cloth Gilt, 1s.

Time Bill, Map and List of Fares, sent free on application to the Owner,

DAVID MACBRAYNE. 119 HOPE STREET, GLASGOW.

The 1885 advert showed a very stylised paddle steamer with a giant paddle box with only five vents, and had the text broken up into sections, making it more readable. It featured *Columba* and *Iona*, day trips by these steamers to Ardrishaig and a week-long trip to Stornoway by *Claymore* or *Clansman*.

SUMMER TOURS IN SCOTLAND.

1910.

THE ROYAL ROUTE.

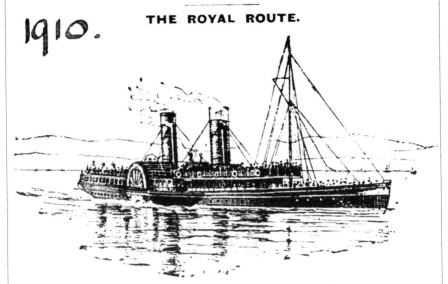

Glasgow and the Highlands

By DAVID MACBRAYNE, Ltd., ROYAL MAIL STEAMERS.

Columba	Gairlochy	Linnet	Claymore	Handa	Texa
Iona	Glengarry	Gael	Cavalier	Cygnet	Mabel
Grenadier	Glencoe	Sheila	Pioneer	Lapwing	Scout
Fusilier	Lochawe	Nellie	Clydesdale	Fingal	Comet
Chevalier	Lochiel	Lochinvar	Dirk	Plover	
Gondolier	Lochness	Chieftain	Ethel	Brenda	

New Steamer—"MOUNTAINEER."

Kyles of Bute, Tarbert, and Ardrishaig,

Conveying Passengers *via* Crinan and Caledonian Canals for

Oban, Staffa and Iona, Ballachulish, Glencoe, Fort William, Fort Augustus, Inverness, Loch Awe, Loch Lomond, Loch Katrine, The Trossachs, Loch Tay, Loch Earn, Loch Scavaig, Loch Coruisk, Mull, Skye, Gairloch, Loch Maree, The Hebrides, Stornoway, Islay, etc.

OFFICIAL GUIDE-BOOK, 6d.
TOURIST PROGRAMME,

Which contains Time Tables, Map, and List of Fares, including all
information regarding

A day's sail to Ardrishaig and back by "Columba" or "Iona," Tours
by the Swift Steamers through the West Highlands, and A Week's
Trip by the "Chieftain," "Claymore," "Cavalier," etc.,
will be sent free on application to the Owners,

By 1910 a much more accurate drawing of *Columba* featured in the advertisement.

STEAMER
AND
MOTOR COACH TOURS
FROM
GLASGOW

For further particulars apply:
DAVID MACBRAYNE Ltd.
44 ROBERTSON STREET, GLASGOW, C.2
Telephone: CENtral 9231   Telegrams: MACBRAYNE

SEASON   1957

The excursion programme from Glasgow for 1957, featuring *Saint Columba*, then in her penultimate season, with a MacBrayne bus. Tours were offered to Ardrishaig by train and steamer, also both ways by bus, and outward by steamer, returning by bus, known as 'The Tour Argyll'. There were also bus return trips to Inveraray Castle, excursions by train and steamer to Staffa and Iona, departing Glasgow Central at 0400, and to Oban via steamer to Ardrishaig, thence bus, returning by train, and by steamer to Tarbert, bus to Campbeltown, returning by steamer.

MACBRAYNE'S STEAMERS

FROM GOUROCK AND TIGHNABRUAICH

CHEAP DAY SAILINGS

BY

R.M.S. SAINT COLUMBA

(or other Steamer)

TO

TARBERT & ARDRISHAIG

(via Kyles of Bute)

(allowing about 1½ hours ashore at Tarbert)

(DAILY EXCEPT SUNDAYS ALL THE YEAR ROUND)

			a.m.				p.m.
GOUROCK	str. dep.		9 30	*ARDRISHAIG	str. dep.		1 00
DUNOON	,,	,,	9 45	TARBERT	,,	,,	1 40
INNELLAN	,,	,,	10 00	TIGHNABRUAICH	,,		2 40
ROTHESAY	,,	,,	10 30	ROTHESAY	,,	,,	3 30
TIGHNABRUAICH	,,		11 10	INNELLAN	,,	,,	3 50
TARBERT	,,		12 0n	DUNOON	,,	,,	4 10
*ARDRISHAIG	,,	arr.	12 45p	GOUROCK	,,	arr.	4 25

✳ Until 28th April and from 1st October, Steamer terminates at Tarbert.

DAY FARES : valid day of issue only

From	To Tighnabruaich (Kyles of Bute) 1st Class s. d.	To Tarbert and Ardrishaig 1st Class s. d.
GOUROCK	7 6	10 0
TIGHNABRUAICH	—	6 0

TICKETS CAN BE OBTAINED FROM THE PURSER ON BOARD THE STEAMER

All Passengers and their Luggage, Goods and Livestock, carried subject to each Company's Conditions of Carriage as specified in Sailing Bills, Notices and Announcements.

MEALS AND REFRESHMENTS ARE AVAILABLE ON BOARD STEAMERS

DAVID MACBRAYNE LTD.

CLYDE HOUSE

44 Robertson Street, Glasgow, C.2   Phone: Central 9231

Custom House Quay,
Greenock
Phone: No. 22834

Season 1956

Pier Office,
Rothesay
Phone: No. 150

A 1956 handbill for the sailing from Gourock to Ardrishaig by *Saint Columba*. Similar handbills were produced for sailings from Dunoon and from Rothesay.

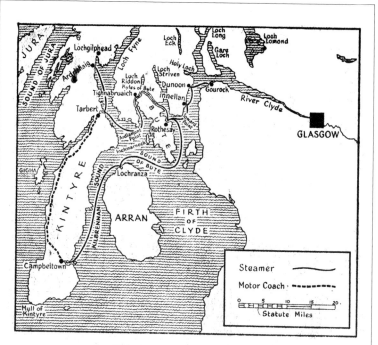

FROM GOUROCK ONLY

KINTYRE CIRCULAR TOUR
(TOUR 3A)

by Steamer and Coach to

KYLES of BUTE, TARBERT and CAMPBELTOWN

on

Mondays, Thursdays and Saturdays
26th MAY to 24th SEPTEMBER, 1956

also on Tuesdays, Wednesdays and Fridays
26th JUNE to 31st AUGUST, 1956

TIME TABLE

GOUROCK	Steamer dep.	9 30 a.m.
TARBERT	,, arr.	12 0 noon
TARBERT	Coach dep.	12 20 p.m.
CAMPBELTOWN	,, arr.	2 10 p.m.
CAMPBELTOWN	Steamer dep.	3 0 p.m.
GOUROCK	,, arr.	7 35 p.m.

First Class   Third Class

Fare   **20/5   18/8***

*Valid on any part of the Steamer from Campbeltown.

TICKETS CAN BE OBTAINED FROM THE PURSER ON BOARD THE STEAMER

The reverse of the previous items features the Kintyre Circular Tour, by *Saint Columba* to Ardrishaig, bus to Campbeltown, and steamer, normally *Duchess of Hamilton*, or on fridays, *Duchess of Montrose*, back to Gourock.

MACBRAYNE'S STEAMERS

Attractive
COACH AND STEAMER TOUR
to
IONA
(THE SACRED ISLE)
on
Fridays only, 12th June to 11th September, 1964
from DUNOON

TIME TABLE

			a.m.				p.m.
DUNOON	Coach	dep.	8.00	IONA	Str.	dep.	3.15
OBAN	Str.	,,	11.15	OBAN	,,	arr.	6.00
			p.m.	OBAN	Coach	dep.	6.00
IONA	,,	arr.	1.45	DUNOON	,,	arr.	8.45
(1½ hours allowed ashore)							

Fare 43/-

Passengers require to book in advance for this tour with
Mr J. McVicar, Craigen Hotel, Argyll Street, Dunoon.

All Passengers and their Luggage, Goods and Livestock carried subject to the Company Conditions of Carriage as specified in Sailing Bills, Notices and Announcements.

MEALS AND REFRESHMENTS ARE AVAILABLE ON BOARD STEAMER

DAVID MACBRAYNE LIMITED
CLYDE HOUSE

44 Robertson Street, Glasgow, C.2.   Phone: CENtral 9231

Local Agent—Mr J. McVicar, Craigen Hotel, Argyll Street, Dunoon.
Phone: No. 307

SEASON 1964

[P.T.O.

A 1964 handbill for a coach and steamer tour to Iona from Dunoon, operated on Fridays in that year when *King George V* started from Fort William and operated to Iona via the south of Mull both ways rather than sailing round Mull as she did for the remainder of the week.

MACBRAYNE'S

STEAMER AND
MOTOR COACH TOURS

FROM

OBAN

For Particulars apply—

DAVID MACBRAYNE LIMITED

North Pier, Oban

Telephone: 2285   Telegrams: **MACBRAYNE**

SEASON 1963

The cover of the Oban excursion programme for 1963, showing the 1955 *Claymore* in a West Highland scene with a MacBrayne bus on a loch-side road. In that year trips were offered to Staffa and Iona Fridays and Sundays excepted, and to Iona Fridays only, both by *King George V. Lochnevis* served Fort William on Mondays, Wednesdays and Fridays, and did Six Lochs cruises on Tuesdays and Thursdays. On Tuesday and Saturdays a return trip to Tobermory was possible, outward by *King George V* and returning in the evening by *Claymore*. Evening trips were offered to Fort William on Mondays, Wednesdays and Fridays and to Salen on Thursdays. Coach and Steamer excursions were offered to Inverness, to Dunoon, using *Lochfyne* from Ardrishaig to Dunoon, returning by coach, and to Glencoe, outward by *Lochnevis* to Fort William, returning by coach.

Map of Route

CRUISE

TO

THE SIX LOCHS

and

Corrievreckan Whirlpool

DAVID MACBRAYNE LTD.

The cover of a descriptive leaflet for the Six Lochs and Corrievreckan whirlpool cruise from Oban, with *King George V* illustrated on the cover, although at that time, *Lochnevis* was the vessel used on the cruise. The six lochs were Loch Melfort, Crinan Loch, Loch Craignish, Loch Buie, Loch Linnhe and Loch Corry.

MACBRAYNE'S STEAMERS

MORNING CRUISES

by

M. V. LOCH EYNORT

from

KYLE OF LOCHALSH

Mondays -	- **LOCH DUICH**
Tuesdays -	- **APPLECROSS & KISHORN**
Wednesdays -	**BROADFORD BAY & RAASAY**
Thursdays -	- **LOCH DUICH**
Fridays -	- **APPLECROSS & KISHORN**
Saturdays -	- **BROADFORD BAY & RAASAY**

Each Cruise Departs at 10.30 a.m. and Arrives back at 12.30 p.m.

CRUISE FARES 7/6 EACH

These cruises will operate subject to there being sufficient demand and to weather and circumstances permitting.

All Passengers and their Luggage, Goods and Livestock, are carried subject to the Company's Conditions of Carriage as specified in Sailing Bills, Notices and Announcements

For further particulars apply:-

DAVID MACBRAYNE LIMITED

Steam Packet Office
KYLE OF LOCHALSH
Phone: 4218

HEAD OFFICE:
CLYDE HOUSE,
1964   **44 ROBERTSON STREET, GLASGOW, C.2.**

PICKERING AND INGLIS LTD., 229 BOTHWELL STREET, GLASGOW, C.2.

An unusual handbill offering morning cruises from Kyle of Lochalsh on *Loch Eynort* in 1964. At this time she was operating the Kyle to Portree service, which arrived at Kyle at 10.15 and departed at 2.45 each day.

A leaflet for the sailings to Islay for 1969, the final year of sailings there before the advent of the car ferry with a drawing of *Lochiel* on the cover. Extra weekend sailings were offered by *Lochnevis*.

FESTIVAL OF THE COUNTRYSIDE

11th to 22nd May 1970
Wester Ross
Ullapool/Gairloch/South West Ross

PRELIMINARY PROGRAMME

Subject to Amendment

**Wester Ross Area Tourist Organisation/
Highlands & Islands Development Board**

Tuesday 19th May

R.M.S. KING GEORGE V CRUISE DAY

dep. Kyle	- 0800	dep. Ullapool	- 1530
arr. Portree	- 0930	arr. Aultbea	- 1700
arr. Aultbea	- 1200	arr. Portree	- 1930*
arr. Ullapool	- 1330	arr. Ullapool	- 2300

* Coach to Kyle from Portree

Inverewe Gardens Open Day—Inverewe
Peat Cutting Demonstration—Inverasdale

Evening Entertainment
Illustrated Talk—Ullapool
Illustrated Talk—South West Ross
Countryside Cinema—Gairloch

Wednesday 20th May

R.M.S. KING GEORGE V CRUISE DAY

dep. Ullapool	- 0900	dep. Tarbert (Harris)	- 1600
arr. Aultbea	- 1030	arr. Aultbea	- 1830
arr. Tarbert (Harris)	1300	arr. Ullapool	- 2000

National Trust Torridon Open Day—Torridon
(including a visit to Deer Museum)
Sheepdog Handling Demonstration—Gairloch
National Trust Kintail Open Day—Kintail
Falls of Glomach Tour via Killilan—
South West Ross Area
Salmon Netting Demonstration—Loch Duich

Evening Entertainment
Barbecue/Folk Singing/Piping—Ullapool
Illustrated Talk—Gairloch
Countryside Cinema—South West Ross Area

Thursday 21st May

R.M.S. KING GEORGE V CRUISE DAY

dep. Ullapool	- 0830	dep. Isle of Handa	- 1500
arr. Aultbea	- 1000	arr. Ullapool	- 1800
arr. Isle of Handa	- 1300	arr. Aultbea	- 1930

Inverpolly Nature Reserve Open Day
Knockan Nature Trail Walking Tour
Beinn Eighe Nature Reserve Open Day—
Kinlochewe
Applecross Day—South West Ross Area
Boat Cruise—Kyle

Evening Entertainment
Barbecue/Folk Singing/Piping and "Open Ship"
Event—Aultbea
Countryside Cinema—Ullapool
Illustrated Talk—South West Ross Area

The programme for a few
days of public charter sailings
by *King George V* to Wester
Ross including calls at Aultbea,
Ullapool, and Tarbet (Harris)
in May 1970. This was part of
the 'Festival of the Countryside'
sponsored by the Highlands
and Islands Development board
and the Wester Ross Area
Tourist Organisation.

The Lewis Mail

Come join us in another song, its theme you'll quickly guess,
We'll journey o'er the Famous Minch, in Norman's trig "Lochness,"
We'll leave the Lewis Capital, when chimes the midnight hour,
Then land you on the pier at Kyle, just as the clock strikes fower.

The men who take this Lewis Mail are seldom long in bed,
But you've to see the way the Steward has got that table spread :
Good ham and egg, then eggs and ham, for dinner broth and meat,
The Minch gives them that appetite, when any food is sweet.

The Captain's from the Mystic Isle, its story he can tell,
His wife, sweet Tobermory Maid, from Mary's Dainty Well ;
He loves the life, adores his wife, and worships his wee daughter,
Great service marks his duty here, each night he's on the water.

The Mate is one named Calum Black, from Muileach's Sunny Isle,
The weather never counts with him, he greets it with a smile ;
Then Jura claims the second mate, son of a worthy sire,
Land of the Paps, the Shaws, and Macs, all men of fame and fire.

The lads that tend "The Coffee Mill" you're safe to call them Mac,
All proud to serve their Noble Chief, who's only lately back,
From far away and distant lands, where once he wandered free,
But now the homeland charms his heart and home he'll ever be.

First Angus takes the wheel awhile, then Calum does his spell,
Don looks the compass in the face, for each one knows it well ;
They joined "Lochness" when she was new, and though the work is hard,
Are proud to take this Lewis Mail and get their rich reward.

When Sandy's gangway doors are tight, the Captain rings "stand by,"
With Finlay at the furrid rope, then Neilly must look spry ;
The wind is blowing fresh to-night and as we pass the Crowlin,
Donald, he gives Chips a hand, sou-west the gale is howlin'.

We're sailing now before the wind and steam is blowing off,
For Johnnie Green's on duty now, the sea is rather rough ;
We? John is sitting down below, while Dan is snug in bed,
For Arnott has the throttle closed, just as the Chief had said.

Now, Ronnie, give that rod some oil, and keep her running sweet,
We'll need our time when running south, when sea and wind we meet ;
Tell Ramage to be handy when we're coming near the Light,
And Stachie keep the burners clean for running south to-night.

A Glasgow Goodbye To The Old Brigade
1864-1878-1935

WE heard it rumoured here and there, but now its quite the truth,
That we must lose two honoured friends, first met in early youth ;
There names were ever household words, well known the country over,
Their pictures graced each station wall, from John o' Groats to Dover.

We'll never see their like again, yet that fame must ever last,
While we would ponder o'er the scenes and pleasures of the past ;
For they were part of Scotland's life, when Glasgow Fair came round,
As boys we met those treasured friends, when to the Highlands bound.

We'd board "Columba" at the Bridge, then start our trip at seven,
This prospect viewed for months ahead, the Royal Route was heaven.
"Iona" left from Tarbert then, when round near Toward they'd meet,
Each with great funnels crimson red, the pride of all the fleet.

The Grand Saloon like Castle Hall, each side yon massive table,
We gathered round that festive board and ate as we were able ;
Breakfast—Herring, Ham and Toast; Lunch—Salmon, Chicken, Pie and Roast,
For we went "Doon the Watter" then, but now it's "To the Coast."

9

In the mid-thirties a number of poems appeared about the demises of some MacBrayne favourites. 'The Clyde, the Columba and the Royal Route' takes us on a trip by *Columba, Linnet, Mountaineer, Fusilier* and *Gondolier* from Glasgow to Inverness via Ardrishaig, the Crinan Canal, Oban and the Caledonian Canal; 'A Glasgow Goodbye to the Old Brigade' celebrates the demise of *Columba* and *Iona*; 'P S *Glencoe* says cheerio to New *Lochfyne*' marks the introduction of *Lochfyne* and the end of the octogenarian *Glencoe*; 'Souvenir of Two Old Favourites' marks the end of *Claymore* and *Glencoe*; 'Claibhmor-slan-leat' marks the last voyage of *Claymore*; and 'The Lewis Mail' a trip on *Lochness*. All were written by the anonymous J.W.

THE CLYDE
THE COLUMBA
AND
THE ROYAL ROUTE

"IONA" The Bonnie, "COLUMBA" The Great,
To see you just passing, how often we'd wait.

R.M.S. "IONA"—1864-1935.

R.M.S. "COLUMBA"—1878-1935.

" No pen could e'er do justice to the varied sights we've seen,
The Mighty Bens, the Heath-clad Hills, with the Waters deep and clean."

Clyde River Steamer Club

Want to find out more about Clyde Steamers?
Why not join the Clyde River Steamer Club
Benefits of membership include:
An annual magazine with historic and modern articles about Clyde Steamers
An annual review of all the happenings in and about Scottish passenger vessels
Monthly illustrated meetings in
Jury's Hotel, 80 Jamaica Street, Glasgow, G1 4QG
from October to April.
Annual subscription only.£16.00
For further information write to
The Secretary, CRSC, 67 Atholl Drive, Giffnock, Glasgow, G45 6QW
www.clyderiversteamerclub.org.uk

West Highland Steamer Club

Want to find out more about West Highland Steamers?
Why not join the West Highland Steamer Club
Benefits of membership include:
A twice-yearly illustrated journal recording the events
of all passenger shipping in the West Highlands
Monthly illustrated meetings in
Renfield St. Stephen's Church Centre, Bath St, Glasgow, G2 4JP
from October to April.
Annual subscription only.£15.00
For further information write to
Mr Robin Love 'Hebrides', 29 Cyprus Avenue, ELDERSLIE, Paisley PA5 9NB.
http://www.loveofscotland.com/whsc/